IF
GOD IS LOVE,
WHY DO I FEEL SO BAD?

Considering Our Images of God

REV. MARCIA COPE FLEISCHMAN

ARPress
ILLUMINATING IDEAS,
EMPOWERING VOICES

ARPress
45 Dan Road Suite 5
Canton MA 02021
Hotline: 1(888) 821-0229
Fax: 1(508) 545-7580

Ordering Information:
Quantity sales. Special discounts are available on quantity purchases by corporations, associations, and others. For details, contact the publisher at the address above.

Printed in the United States of America.

ISBN-13:   Softcover   979-8-89330-505-0

                eBook   979-8-89330-506-7

Library of Congress Control Number: 2024900442

Table of Contents

Section IV : The Forgotten Image

Section V : New Images of Jesus and God

Section VI : New Images of The Trinity

Section VII : New Mission

DEDICATION

This Book is Dedicated to

Paul Smith

My visionary teacher
Mentor
Co-Pastor
Partner in Ministry
And
Friend

INTRODUCTION

We All Have to Start Somewhere

In our journey with God, we all have to start somewhere.

It is said that God is love. So, do you feel loved by God?

Do you feel that you are a loving gift from God to the world or do you feel bad, sinful, unworthy? Piglet and Pooh were talking one day. Pooh asked Piglet, "Piglet, how do you spell 'love'?"

Piglet responded, "Oh, Pooh, you don't spell love, you feel it!"

For me God is like that. God is to be felt, not spelled, not just talked about, not just sung about.

Do you feel loved by God? Do you feel it; do you know it in your soul. Or are you asking yourself, "If God is love and loves me, how come I feel so bad?"

Did you grow up in a Christian community that followed the "I am a worm" theology? Were you taught to feel bad about yourself? Did you tell yourself "I'm not worthy to be loved by God?

I was picking up a soda at McDonald's the other day. As I reached for my ice-cold drink, the woman in the window, when I asked her how she was said, "I am blessed!" I agreed. I am too. Then she said, "We're not worthy to be blessed." I objected and said, "Yes we are because God loves us."

Right then, right there she was espousing the "I am a worm theology…I'm not worthy to be loved by God." How sad this is for someone to carry such a huge burden of self-doubt and shame around in her heart. How did we learn to feel this way about ourselves? How did we learn to think this badly of ourselves? Part of the reason, I've come to believe is that we imag*ine* and/or have been taught that God doesn't like us. We have been taught that we are sinful and unworthy. The Christian theology has endorsed the concept of "original sin" and helped us develop an image of God that reinforces this belief.

In the movie *Wayne's World, the* main characters, Wayne and Garth, meet the famous rock star, Alice Cooper. They get down on their knees and bow to him chanting "We're not worthy! We're not worthy!" Many people enter church or quiet time or prayer time feeling deeply in their hearts…" I'm not worthy! I'm really not worthy!"

Is this you?

If so, it's time to investigate what is behind that belief about yourself. It could be that it is partly because you have been taught or have come to believe on your own that God is more ogre than kind, more monster than mothering, more shaming than healing, more sinister than saving.

One of the first times I was given an opportunity to question what God was actually like was in the class I took, almost every Saturday for a year, to prepare to join my church, the Communicants Class.

It was in this class that I caught a glimpse of something else, a different way of seeing God and our connection with God. We were studying the Westminster Catechism, a teaching tool to help students understand the general beliefs of the church. The format was that there was a question presented and "the answer". Each of us had to memorize one of the questions and the answer. The day we joined the church (which was a Palm Sunday) we had to state the question and answer in front of the congregation. I clearly remember my question:

"What is the chief end of man {supposedly a gender-inclusive term at the time}?

Answer: "The chief end of man is to glorify God and enjoy God forever."

I had taken this answer to heart and spent years trying to answer this question, to make this answer my own, to make this answer alive in my life. But how do we actually glorify and enjoy God?

I started pursuing God at that point. The pursuit has been the journey of my life. The biggest part of the journey was to discover what God looked like and felt like to me. I learned as I went along that we each carry images of God within us and that image creates our spiritual journey.

So, come on a journey with me. It is an inner journey through myths and monsters, images and imaginings, musings and mysteries, through joys and sorrows. We will follow a path of different images of God, illustrations that I have created over years of studying what people think God looks like. They are images taken from Scriptures, people's imaginations, from urban legend, books and podcasts. And some images that I made up myself. I ask you to get in touch with your image, or images of God.

We need to climb the mountains of disbelief and swim the murky waters of fear-engendering images of a manipulating, punishing, angry God. We will open our hearts to a kind, loving and nurturing God. The destination is to find and enjoy God and for God to enjoy us. The ultimate goal is for each or us, and, yes, you, gentle reader, to feel loved by God.

For that journey to happen we need to dig deep, be honest about how we think and feel about God and to stretch, stretch, stretch ourselves to grow and change. This is a chance to find how your personal image of God influences your life and impacts your participation in the world.

The book that spoke to me most and inspired my looking for images of God was *Good Goats, Bad Goats* by Denis, Mathew and Sheila Linn. Denis tells of a turning point in his journey with and understanding of God:

As God became more loving to me, I became more loving.

Denis's realization was what we call a spiritual awakening. His realization was that he reflected into the world what his inner image of God was. If he saw God as judgmental and condemning, he was judgmental and condemning. As his healing journey progressed, he experienced the love of God. His image of God changed to become a loving. When he saw God as loving, he became more loving. His reflection of God in the world was love.

Our spiritual journey toward knowing God happens with many awakenings. With each awakening, also called epiphany, we get to know more and more about the God we seek. Like the story of the blind men describing an elephant from different viewpoints. One man feels the elephant's trunk and says he is like a giant hose. One man feels the elephant's tail and says it looks like a rope. One feels the elephant's leg and says he looks like a tree trunk and so on. We each see different aspects of God.

Part of the process of emotional healing and growth involves surfacing our subconscious thoughts and feelings, bringing them to the surface into our awareness. What are your thoughts about God? More importantly, for this journey, what are your feelings about God. I hope this book is an opportunity to explore many aspects of the Creator and how you feel about God. Journaling about thoughts and feelings helps bring you into the awareness your internal processes and drivers of your spiritual life.

This will be a chance for you to journal and even sketch your ideas, digging deeper into how God feels to you. So, you ask, how will we travel on this journey? We will travel on some images of God that I have created. This journal will give you the opportunity to express your ideas and experiences about God. It will be fun to see where you go, where you learn, where you stretch and how you might change.

Yes, you can change your life by how you relate to God.

I will explain more about myself as tour guide.

The journey started for me around 5th grade when I first began to wonder about God. I first wondered what church was about. I was old enough to not sit under the pew and color and draw anymore. One day, I was sitting in the pew, pouting. Apparently, I was mad about something and I sat at the end of the pew with my lip stuck out, quietly listening. In a fit of reverse psychology my mother praised my grownup behavior, my listening to the sermon. That praise changed me and I started to pay attention.

That was the beginning of a life long journey toward God. I began to wonder if there was something more to the journey with God. Was there anything more? Was it just about dressing up one a week and going to church?

At Christmas my mom set up her old Nativity set in the dining room on the tall cherry wood antique sideboard. There was a tiny light shining down from the wooden creche, illuminating the figures of Mary, Joseph and baby Jesus in his straw filled manager. I was drawn to the scene as that little light shone over Jesus in the darkened dining room of my home. I stood there wondering what was the story of Jesus all about. I had no clue.

In the summer that year I went to Vacation Bible School. That year several churches joined forces in my small town and we were the oldest class. We had a special teacher, Miss Eva Saunders. Everyone called her Miss Eva. She was a large, older African American woman who was a pillar of the whole community. During class, Miss Eva would break out in song, praising God. Even more amazing to me, she talked about God like she knew God. I was fascinated. I guess I could say it was my first epiphany of God. She was the only person I ever met who talked about God like she knew God. Everyone else just talked about what they thought about God.

Where did your journey begin?

After these revelations, I muddled along, not thinking much about God. I was just involved with growing up. Then, my junior year in college, I went to study in France for the year. While I was away the boyfriend I left behind and my best girl friend since 6tth grade wrote that they had connected with God through giving their lives to Jesus.

What?

People all over the America were accepting Jesus as their Lord and Savior. He was changing their lives with his love. In the 1970s it was called the Jesus Movement. When I returned home it was obvious to me that I would lose a boyfriend and a friend if I didn't say yes to Jesus. So; I did. It may have been a very shallow and somewhat insincere way of making a commitment to God. I hardly knew that making a commitment was what I was doing. Somehow God must had heard the long-time cry of my heart and accepted that shallow prayer.

I went to a retreat that October and heard one of the leaders talk about God as if she knew God. In my soul, I realized that I had already stepped onto the road that would take me to that same place. Eventually, I would find God and get to know God. I would, at some point, experience God and God's love for me.

That weekend, God's love broke through to me. I felt loved, for the first time. In retrospect I realized that I had suffered depression all my life. That depression kept love out. I had never felt loved. I knew my family loved me but I didn't feel loved.

Then, on that wonderful retreat in October, I felt loved. For the first time. I felt loved by God, my Creator! I was ecstatic and my life began to change

Skip forward a few years. I was 24.

I married a man, Ken (not the boyfriend in college) who wanted to pursue knowing God, too. He found a church In Kansas City where we lived called Broadway (Baptist at the time) Church and was loving called "Broadway" by the members. And guess what, they talked like they knew God there. I was home and found a wonderful journey to God through the teaching there.

A big emphasis of the teaching at Broadway Church was about following a healing path in one's life through both the loving presence of God in our lives and through the process of psychotherapy. Transactional Analysis was all the rage and we began to be aware of our psychological journey, the wounds and gifts of our lives and how to heal. Church was about transforming our lives!

Many people at Broadway were in therapy and my husband and I sought our own healing process. We were learning about Transactional Analysis at the time. We learned about the ego states of Parent, Adult, Child. Even more we learned about the Critical Parent, Nurturing Parent, Adaptive Child and Rebellious Child. I bring this up as it explains so much to me about how we relate to God. Do you relate to God as Child to Parent, as Adult to Adult or as adaptive or rebellious Child to Critical Parent? There are many possibilities.

Through the teachings at Broadway, especially through the teachings of Paul Smith, the main teaching Pastor, I learned about healing and God's love. In fact, I had never heard anyone teach about God's love like Paul did. I was healing from old hurts just listening to his teaching and through worship. It was is worship that I began to feel God's presence. Then Paul taught about the beginning of mysticism, Christian mysticism. Paul taught us how to tune in and listen to God speaking to us. It was marvelous!

Listening to God was a big step forward into the mystical journey. It is about experiencing God's presence. It is the way Jesus related to God. I began to realize that the experiential aspect of following Jesus had been the raging desire of my heart. I wanted to know God the way Jesus did. Through the practice of tuning into the Holy Spirit and enjoying the Presence of God for over 20 years, I, now, I consider myself a mystic, a Christian mystic.

Being a Christian mystic means I am more interested in the experience of God than in the dogma and belief systems of the religion or the churches. I learned how to tune into God, the Spirit and Jesus. God became so real to me and I needed some debunking and healing from my previous life experiences.

When I studied theology in Seminary, I was more interested in what God was like, how God interacted with people, how God changed people's lives. I was more interested in the transformative presence of God's love. And I wanted to know how God felt to other people in their experiences.

I was on the Healing Prayer Team at church. The church staff taught about healing prayer, both how to give healing prayer and how to receive healing prayer.

We had famous teachers on healing prayer come and speak and pray for us. The speakers were Tommy Tyson, a Methodist evangelist, Fr. Francis McNutt, a Charismatic Catholic priest, Brennon Manning, Denis, Matthew and Sheila Linn, Dominican Catholics.

One night after Tommy Tyson and Francis McNutt had taught about healing prayer, everyone that wanted to be prayed for lined up in front of the church and the two teachers and our senior pastor, Paul Smith, walked down the line touching our shoulders or heads lightly and praying in their prayer language. Most of us fell over, were caught and laid gently on the floor. It happened to me. It is called Resting in the Spirit and what an experience it was!

I was totally enfolded by the love of God. I was relaxed and aware of my surroundings, but at the same time totally blissed out. Then a funny thing happened. A stream of energy was flowing over me, from head to foot. I was lying on my back and somehow was kind of tucked up under the front pew. The stream of energy was like a babbling brook flowing over me and it made me laugh. I laughed out loud. Then I laughed some more. Then the whole audience (those left that remained sitting) started laughing too. I remember thinking, "Are they laughing at me?" I thought, "No, that couldn't be." Because I felt like I was 2 blocks away. But they were and the laughter went on like that for a while, first me and then them. It was a most amazing experience and a deepening of my experience of God. I have had the same experience several times. Both resting and laughing in the Spirit. I know that God can feel like pure joy, pure bliss. And God makes me laugh!

As I got prayed for and the healing process continued, I began to pray for others. God would give me pictures in my head that I was meant to share with the person we were praying for. I began an astounding time of prayer and getting to know God in those prayer times. I would say that praying for others is where I really got to see God work in peoples' lives. I got to know what God was like and how God felt about and thought about us, His beloveds.

When people prayed for me, I got pictures for myself. For a long time, I thought it would be fun to paint the pictures I was given, to bring spiritual images into reality. Then, after a double lung transplant, I started to paint.

I became an artist later in my life. I was very sick for 5.5 years from taking a bad medication and my only way out of death was a very tricky and dangerous double lung transplant. I was transplanted in February 2003. A volunteer at the hospital taught some acrylic painting techniques to the transplant survivors and spouses during our free time while we were in our three-month rehabilitation.

I had to live in St. Louis where I received my new lungs and continued rehab. I returned to my home in Kansas and resumed my life on staff at Broadway Church. We were raising money to remodel the kitchen which had not changed since 1932. I suggested I could paint images of angels and sell them to raise money for the remodeling. I tell the amazing story of that adventure in my book *Angels I Have Seen.* I continue to paint angels for people from imagesthat pop into my head. So now I have painted images of God that we will consider on our journey.

From this journey I hope you will be able to do the following:

- Journal about your journey with God.
- Open your mind and spirit to embrace different images of God
- Experience more of the love of God
- Heal from old, harmful images and beliefs about God
- Become aware of the subconscious influences that an image of God can achieve

I invite you to participate as fully as you can to journal and draw throughout this book. Please, feel free to draw stick figures to express your ideas. It's a journal and no one is watching!

Let's start at the very beginning. Our parents are usually our first impression of God. They are our creators; they are our first experience of God. Keep them in mind as you consider your first impressions of God, of your first internal images, how you imagined God to be.

I invite to on a journey of discovery, discovering how you picture God in your mind, discovering if you want to engage with a God like your image, discovering new ways to imagine and relate to God.

SECTION I

Urban Legends of God

Surfing the Urban Legends

Much of what we hear about God comes from stories we've heard. We form images of God that aren't really based on anything official like teaching from Holy writings, serious theological study, or even revelation. We form pictures from snippets of conversations or phrases people drop into conversations.

The first image is one that I held as true and I still find people that see God this way: The Old Man in the Sky with a Long, White Beard.

I asked a friend about what she thought God looked like. This was her answer. She had advanced degrees in her field and had a wonderful, vital career. She was a life-long church goer and believer. However, she had not really considered what God actually might look like. Notice in this painting that God seems rather benign, happy, lover of animals and kites. He seems happy and non-threatening. This is what I would call an urban legend. It is a widely held belief that isn't discovered or questioned. This image of God feels distant and not involved in our lives, just up there in the sky, hanging out.

"God is in His heaven and all is right with the world" This is a famous quote from Robert Browning poem "Pippa Passes." It is Pippa, a little Italian girl that sings this phrase. The poem was written in by Browning in 1841. It is a phrase still used often and helps to develop this passive image of a benign, non-threatening, uninvolved God.

Take a moment to write about how this image affects you. How does God feel to you? How would you draw this God?

CHAPTER 1

The One We Talk To

When you are distressed, sad and lonely, who do you talk to? Perhaps you talk to a spouse, a friend, family members. How about when you are all alone. There is no one there and yet you need to talk. Perhaps you talk to God, intentionally or even accidentally. Talking to God is called prayer. Prayer is talking to God.

I lived through the 1960s. One of the trials and also one of the gifts of the 60s was that everything seemed to be in upheaval. Old ideas, old beliefs, traditions and practices were thrown out, rejected. Everything was up for debate and scrutiny. New things were being tried. Even fashion was changing.

One outstanding example that I'll never forget was the dress code at my small Midwest Methodist college. We were told that we could only wear skirts on campus. We could only wear skirts downtown shopping, although it was just a small town.

If we wanted to wear pants to the library, it had to be formal slacks. Jeans were forbidden. I don't know what boys were supposed to wear, just not jeans.

Then, my junior year I went to study in Strasbourg, France, for the entire year. A friend there worked for a newspaper and he showed us a story and photos from the Kent State riot. That included a now famous photo of a young woman kneeling over the body of a stain student. It was chaos, the winds of change.

When I got back to campus, everyone was wearing jeans all the time, guys and gals. Everyone.

It was a time of great upheaval and questioning and rejecting. Everything was changing. People were even changing how they thought about God and how they talked to God. People were talking about how to pray.

Conversational prayer came on the scene. Until then, if you grew up in church, the way of praying seemed to always be formal, sometimes using the archaic language of "Thee" and "Thou". It was a cumbersome affair. Some Christian establishments had prayer books. They contained formal prayers, too. The message was clear, this is the way to pray.

Jesus apparently felt the need of his followers concerning how to pray. "This is how you do it." Said Jesus. And he recited the Lord's Prayer: it went like this:

Our Father, which art in Heaven hallowed be thy name.

Thy Kingdom come; Thy will be done on Earth as it is in Heaven

Give us this day our daily bread and forgive us our debts as we forgive our debtors.

Lead us not into temptation, but deliver us from evil.

For thine is the kingdom, and the power, and the glory forever. Amen

In case you are wondering, different denominations of different churches have differing versions. I grew up in a Presbyterian church so this is the prayer I learned.

With these stunning examples of how to pray, it is amazing that any of us mere mortals even took a chance at praying.

Someone along the line, having mastered the crux of conversational prayer, introduced one of my favorite prayers. It goes like this:

"Lord, HELP!"

But conversational Prayer broke all the barriers. It goes like this:

"You can talk to God like you talk to anyone else."

Yes, it is that simple. But how does it happen? Here are some stories that show how some people pray.

Seal Team Six

A man who served in the Seal Team Six, an extraordinarily advanced trained Special Forces group, shared his experience on a television show. He said something like this: first that he is not especially religious, but when he was on the field and bullets are swooshing by his head at 3000 miles per hour, he started praying, praying to whoever is out there. He said, I don't care who it is. I prayed to whoever would listen.

Praying, or talking to whoever is out there seems, for him, to be a very natural thing to do.

Prayers of a 4-year-old

A friend, Bev, shared her story. She was a little girl living with her single mom who had a boyfriend. When the boyfriend came over to visit, my friend would go sit on the curb and play.

She also remembered going to a little church down the street. She really liked it and especially Sunday School. She liked Sunday School because they had candy and she could eat all she wanted which was a special treat. Her mom certainly could not afford anything as frivolous as candy. And she recounted that they must have taught her to pray.

She remembered praying when she was 4 years old. It seems that, when her mother broke up with her boyfriend, he was enraged. He broke in the house and shot her mother with a shotgun. The little girl ran to her favorite play place on the curb. She sat and prayed to God on the curb asking that her mom would be ok. She had seen so much blood when her mother was shot. She prayed again when she was in court testifying that, yes, he was the man who killed her mother. She learned in Sunday school, even as a little girl, that God was there with her and she could talk to God.

I remember talking to God a lot when I was young.

One of the horrible "have to" projects for us was getting ready to join the church. The process was a class at church that went on for a whole year, once a week. It was the Communicants class. I actually enjoyed most of it. I was learning about God. In the Communicants class, we 5th and 6th graders learned about God and the Westminster Catechism. We each had to teach a lesson. I chose to teach about a hymn that I liked called "Sweet Hour of Prayer." I apparently had been praying as a child and found that talking to God was comforting to me. I knew I was talking to God, whoever I thought God was at the time. And I knew that I was comforted.

Our minister, who was teaching the class, told me that my lesson was very inspired, whatever that meant. Was he talking about being inspired by God? I had no idea what he was saying or what he meant. Most of all prayer, talking to God, was a great comfort to me.

I have been to so many seminars and talks that I don't always remember who said what or when so I could give them credit. I remember stories most of all. I believe it was Brennan Manning who relayed this story in a presentation at Broadway Church many years ago. It is about prayer, talking to God.

Two old men had been friends for many years. One day they were talking when the one said, "I don't know how to pray. How do you pray?" His friend said, "Its easy. You set two chairs opposite each other. You sit in one chair and have Jesus sit in the other. Then you talk to him and then you listen to what he has to say."

"Ok," said the friend and off he went to try it out.

Several years later the old man got sick and was bedridden. He was staying at his daughter's home. She complained to a friend that her dad had a strange habit. He left an empty chair by his bed and he wouldn't let anyone sit in it. One day she had to run some errands and go the grocery store. She first went to check on her dad to see if there was anything he needed. No, he was fine. When she returned about an hour later, she went in to check on him. He had passed away peacefully while she was away.

"Its funny," she said to her friend. "Apparently, just before he died, he leaned over and put his head on that empty chair."

To him, Jesus had become very real as they talked and he listened. Prayer had become, for him, a conversation with Jesus, who Christians consider God in human form. It was Jesus who was sitting on the empty chair.

In my experience of pastoring for over 30 years, it seems to me that most of us don't have to be taught how to pray, at least not at first. It comes naturally. We have to talk to someone and God is who we choose. I am not the only one to observe this. Pascal, the French writer and philosopher observed,

"There is a God-shaped vacuum in the heart of each man (person) which cannot be satisfied by any created thing but only by God the Creator, made known through Jesus Christ."

And so, in the beginning of this book about God, we start with the idea that God is the One we talk to.

Do you talk to God? Write about your experience here.

_____

_____

_____

_____

_____

CHAPTER 2

The Old Man in the Sky

One day I was visiting with Joyce, the nurse for my beloved pulmonologist. We usually have a minute or two to chat after my check- up. I was researching my book and seeking to find peoples' ideas of what God looks like. So, I asked her.

"He looks like an old man in the sky with a long white beard," she replied.

This is a very common answer that I have heard many times over my lifetime. It is in the category of urban legend because it is a commonly held belief that is not founded on any church teaching. It is not based on any Scripture but is picked up in masculine pronouns used for God and the assumption that God is very old. It is a very safe image for the Great Mystery that lingers over us. It is also based on the premise that God looks like we do, so in this representation, God Is White. God is Old and God is Male.

The image of the Old Man in the Sky that I have painted, is actually a picture of a very benign old man. Notice that, being in the sky, the Old Man is far away where he cannot hurt anyone and definitely too far away to contact or connect with. He loves animals, flying kites and watches the Space Shuttle flying by. It is reminiscent of the verse drama written by Robert Browning, "Pippa Passes" in which Pippa sings a song ending with this phrase:

"God's in his Heaven. All's right with the world."

Many people remain disengaged with God through their entire lives and like it that way. It may feel safer, but it also keeps a person separated and away from the love and joy God can provide.

Is this your concept of God? If so, how did you arrive at this conclusion. Explain here:

_____

_____

_____

_____

_____

_____

_____

_____

_____

_____

_____

_____

_____

_____

_____

_____

_____

_____

_____

_____

_____

_____

Is this your concept of God? If so, how did you arrive at this conclusion. Explain here:

CHAPTER 3

The Angry God in the Sky

A new worship pastor at our church told a friend that the members of the congregation practiced listening to God. That we could hear God speaking. What did his friend think about that? He said, "I don't even want God to know where I am, much less have him talk to me!"

That leads us to our second urban legend, the angry God in the sky that is ready to throw lightning bolts at us humans if we transgress. This is a very familiar image of God. I remember feeling His presence very early on.

In the TV series, "The Golden Girls," a story about four older women sharing a house and their lives together. Dorothy, who was played by Bea Arthur, had a favorite saying that she used often, "God's going to get you for that!" That phrase usually got a laugh from the audience. But was it really funny? Underlying the saying was a belief that God was watching us so He could punish us.

Another frequently used saying is, "God's going to strike me with lightening for saying that!" How does that really feel inside. How does it affect our image of God?

A sermon preached by the Rev. Jonathan Edwards on July 8, 1741 was entitled "Sinners in the Hands of an Angry God." Whew, that scares me just to write it down. These ideas of an angry God have been part of our culture for many years.

An anecdote from my college years described how many of us felt about God. It goes like this: God, looking over his balcony in heaven yells, "Hey, you down there!"

"Yes, Lord?"

"Are you having fun?" "Yes, Lord, I am."

"Well, cut it out!"

Seems that God is a real killjoy

Take a moment to write about a time in your life when you have felt the presence of an angry God. Be specific. What did you think God was angry about?

_____

_____

_____

What does angry God's face look like?

_____

_____

_____

_____

_____

_____

_____

_____

_____

_____

_____

_____

_____

_____

_____

_____

_____

_____

CHAPTER 4

God as Santa Claus

Many people think God is like Santa Claus. We ask for things and God gives them or not. Some people don't even think about God until they want something. Sometimes we want to bargain with God.

"God, if you get me out of this jam, I will quit smoking (drinking, gambling, messing around.)"

How many of us wrote letters to Santa Claus asking for the latest toy or something we really wanted?

Many people ask God for things and then are really disappointed when they don't get what they want. This is a rather superficial way of praying and there are many ways to pray and many levels of prayer. If the person doesn't get what he wants, he may refuse to believe in God, be disappointed and reject God.

When my husband had his hemorrhagic stroke, I asked for people to pray for him. That's all I wanted. I asked everyone that reached out to me, "Please, pray."

I knew then that whatever happened it would be ok. Because I believe we all move into the full Presence of God when we die. I knew that whether Ken lived or died, it would be alright.

I got a letter from a special person who said he had been prepared to offer me love and support but when I asked for prayer, he didn't know what to do. That was because his experience taught him that prayer doesn't work.

That was curious for me. He lives at a distance and it wasn't the kind of thing I would just call him about. But this is the origin of this painting, God as Santa Claus. Some people only go to God to ask for something and, when they don't get "it", whatever it may be, or "it" doesn't happen as they wish, they assume that prayer doesn't work.

Is this an image that you have had of God? I still remember asking Santa Claus for a baby reindeer one year and I didn't get it. I never asked for one again.

Have you had this experience of asking for something and your prayer wasn't granted? Write about it.

Is God like Santa Claus? Write what you think.

CHAPTER 5

The God of Don'ts

As I was painting images of God for this book there is one image that came roaring back to me from my past. I will call it "The God of Don'ts." Another way of saying it, this is the God of Rules.

Notice in the painting, the road to God is full of rules. And God is a long way off.

My friend since Kindergarten, Ginny, shared with me that in her image of God he carries around a little black book to write down all our mistakes. She saw the God of Don'ts, too.

Where did this image come from? Why did I feel like and act like it was so real? Because it was very real to me.

I suspect it was the teachings from church that formed this image. The 10 Commandments, straight from the mouth of God to the tablets of Moses, were there for everyone to see, to memorize, for everyone to take to heart. And take it to heart I did. I can remember sitting in the choir loft listening to the sermons. This propaganda about God was reinforced by watching the movie, The Ten Commandments, starring Charlton Heston.

Sadly, in our small town, it usually took 2 years for the new, hot movies to come to our small theatre. I was of dating age by the time Charlton and his crew arrived on Main Street. I was asked on a date to see the movie for Saturday night. Then, someone else asked me to the movie for Friday night. I said yes to both dates as there was little else to do for fun in town. Four hours each night the dramatic presentation of the receiving of THE LAW was played out before my eyes.

If the preacher hadn't succeeded in implanting the "Don'ts of God" into my impressionable little mind, heart and soul, the movie did. I was convinced that the only way to God was by obeying the rules. And the biggest rule for me was…DON'T HAVE SEX!

Around that time, I procured a boyfriend, a steady boyfriend. We didn't "go steady." I liked to keep my options open. But we went steadily. I learned from him what "making out" was all about. What a wonderful discovery! It was a favorite activity for most of us Juniors and Seniors.

Our town was surrounded by corn, wheat and bean fields and the steady couples would find that special spot to be alone together. We all knew the country roads very well. So that was Saturday night, then came Sunday morning and facing God. Oh, how guilty I felt, guilty for necking, guilty for breaking the rule, or getting close to breaking the rule. When I went to college, I learned that most of my friends had experienced the same thing, necking and guilt. We had disappointed God. Oh, the Guilt, oh, the shame, oh, the rules!

When our youngest daughter, Sarah, graduated from college, she got a job in the city, the big bad city, New York City. One day she decided she wanted to check out churches. I suggested a fairly mild church from a mainline denomination. She went to visit. When she returned, she called me on the phone,

"Mom", she demanded, "What's all this about our being sinners?"

Sarah had grown up at Broadway Church and had never heard such stuff. We didn't teach about sin. We all felt bad enough already. We were a healing community. We wanted to heal from the hurts, the shame, the rules.

It seems, sometimes, that the Church needs to make us feel bad in order to "save" us. And the church offers the only way to be saved. As Mathew Fox declares, we are the Original Blessing, not the source of Original Sin. It can take a lot of healing to open these old spiritual wounds in order to feel God's love.

It takes a lot of work to get over the guilt from the God of Don'ts, the God of Rules.

If this image fits for you, write down what you think the rules were and do you still see it that way?

_____

_____

_____

Was there a particular rule that you, for sure, didn't want to break?

_____

_____

_____

Have the rules changed? What are they now? Did you obey the rules, or break them? How did this image affect your relationship with God?

_____

_____

_____

_____

_____

_____

_____

_____

CHAPTER 6

The Puppet Master

This image depicts God controlling all things, people's movements, events, natural disasters like tornados. Many people describe God as the one who pulls the strings like a puppet master, or the one who controls and enlivens marionettes. Marionettes are us!

Recently I saw a picture of the aftermath of a tornado. Hundreds of trees surrounding an old farm house had been flattened by a twister, but the house remained intact, untouched by the wind. The neighbor's house was completely destroyed.

I could imagine the conversation. "God was with us, totally protected us." What does that mean for the neighbors? God wasn't with them? Why not? Why was their house destroyed?

Or, "Our team won because God is on our side." What does that mean for the other team? God wasn't on their side. God made them lose?

Or there are the strange images of God expressed when we try to comfort people in their loss.

Someone dies and we say the strangest things: "God needed him/her in heaven." God doesn't need us? God needed him more than we do?

"Only the good die young!" What does that mean for us, as we are approaching the age of 'older than dirt'?

"God needed another angel in heaven." Do people really turn into angels when they die?

"I know something good will come of this tragedy." I must not trust God since I'm not happy about losing my loved one.

Most of us know not to say these things to people who are grieving a loss, but others haven't figured that out yet. My point is, what do these things say about God? Is God mean, punishing, vindictive, heartless or vengeful?

Why do bad things happen to good people?

A Bible verse addresses some of this:

"He causes his sun to rise on the evil and the good, and sends rain on the righteous and the unrighteous." Matthew 5;45 NIV

Have you ever thought that God was in control of all the events in your life? If so, how did you feel about God and his control?

_____

_____

_____

How would you confront and change this image of God?

_____

_____

_____

_____

_____

_____

_____

_____

_____

_____

_____

_____

_____

_____

_____

_____

_____

_____

_____

_____

CHAPTER 7

The Judge

"Here come de Judge! Here come de Judge! Everyone in da courtroom, here come de Judge."

This was the opening to a skit on a comedy show several years ago. It depicted a courtroom where some funny things happened. I can't remember the skits but I sure remember this line.

Most of us, however, don't think of a Judge or courtroom as funny. Judging is serious business. God as Judge is even more serious.

The problem with God as Judge is that we don't go to a courtroom to find him. We carry him around in our heads. And he is a severe Judge. He fits right into that space in our psyches where we criticize and condemn ourselves.

It is said that the things we say to ourselves are worse than anything we would say to anyone else, even our worst enemies. But we don't hesitate to talk to ourselves in this negative, critical, demanding way.

The story goes that Satan bangs us over the head with a 2 x 4 when we do something wrong. After that he gives us the board and we keep hitting ourselves. It's not that I believe in an actual Satan, but we could even say that it feels like it is God, the Judge, that hits us over the head. Then we carry the internal Judge ever after.

I grew up in a home where my father was very intense. He was a surgeon and I guess that is how they are. It is very demanding and stressful work. I picked up the internal pressure that he felt and applied it to myself. I was a perfectionist and demanded perfection of me. Talk about carrying the internal Judge. I was really competitive and got all As on my grade card for 2-3 years. I finally decided that this kind of life was not much fun and relaxed a tiny bit. In my 20s I entered therapy. As a counselor myself, a master's level school counselor, it was a blow to my ego to submit myself to therapy. The whole church was learning about the healing path of therapy and there were therapy groups called Growth Groups that we could join. My husband and I joined different groups so as not to compete with each other.

On day in group, my therapist said to me "Marcia, it's not 'if you make a mistake,' it's 'when you make a mistake'." I was horrified! How could he possibly mean that I could be so faulty as to make mistakes? That is how strong my inner critic, my inner Judge was. The therapists were so kind, so accepting and so loving. Love is very healing. That's one of the strongest reasons to pursue finding the God who is Love.

I'll never forget the first time I said a non-critical, non-judging comment to myself. I was in our garage cleaning up sawdust from a project Ken and I were working on. I got a huge dustpan full of sawdust and turned around to put it in the garbage can. When I turned, I hit the side of the can with the dustpan and, boom, all the sawdust fell back on the floor. I heard a voice say, "That's ok!" I literally turned around to see who had said such a thing. Then I realized it was me! I had said something nice, kind, loving, forgiving, comforting to myself in just two words. "It's ok."

My life started to change. I very slowly started throwing off the comfortable cloak of criticism. I had a very long road ahead, but I had started the path of kindness to myself. Healing from the past and from myself, from the Critical Parent that lived in me had begun.

After all these years I have come to believe that God does not judge us. Our lives are not about obeying the rules or following the straight and narrow path. Our lives are about learning. God is not a judge but a teacher who works to create goodness in every struggle, in every endeavor. With our goal of being a loving and kind person, we move toward kindness for others. The kindness begins with being kind to ourselves.

List some places in your life where you have felt judged by people and/or God or yourself.

List some times you have judged yourself. What do you judge yourself about?

_____

_____

_____

Take time to write some positive affirmations that would counter the negative, hurtful messages you give yourself.

_____

_____

_____

Repeat these phrases: I am doing the best I can. I am enough. I am learning. I am kind to myself and others.

_____

_____

_____

_____

_____

_____

_____

CHAPTER 8

Watcher

My lifelong friend, Shari, shared this image with me as we were discussing God. She said, "I see God like a mist that watches over us." In this image I show a purple cloud-like substance floating above a group of people. Notice that some people are looking at the cloud, acknowledging its existence. Others are walking along just minding their own business.

The thing that speaks to me about this picture is that Shari did not speak of God as a person but as a mist. God moves out of the limited presence that a body represents. That is a more expansive image of God.

Many of the attributes that we have a difficult time understanding don't seem to work when God is limited by a human-like body. In the classic theologies I studied in Seminary, the attributes

{which were fun to study since I was most interested in what God is like} included things like omnipresent. That means that God is everywhere, with us all the time. Omniscient, God knows everything. Omnipotent, God is all powerful. We learn the important aspects about God but wrestle with how to fit that into a human-like body.

Voltaire said, "God created man in His image, and man returned the favor."

Man changed God into a human-like being with a body. Then we see God as a limited human being. How can one person know all, see all and be all powerful. Our imaginations can't stretch that far. It leads to great misunderstandings of the nature of God. We will discuss this in a later chapter.

Another aspect of God that Shari includes in this image is that God is watching us. Is this good news? Is it bad news? It depends. Does God watch us to enjoy us, or is God watching us to judge and criticize us?

I learn about God by being with my grandchildren. I find I can be all consumed and delighted by watching my grandsons play and interact. You never know what they will say and do. It is fun and joyful! Is God joyful while watching us? Or is God carrying his little black book (Ginny's idea) to keep track of our mistakes, to judge us.

In the bad or good scenario, we have a chance to project onto God the way we are. Projection is seeing in someone else, in this case God, what we know is true about ourselves. A man criticizes his wife of infidelity when it is actually, he that is unfaithful. A woman accused a friend of lying because, actually, it is she who is lying. We project onto God what we believe about ourselves. God thinks I'm bad because I think I'm bad.

Also, in this picture, some people are noticing and perhaps engaging with God, others are oblivious. Are you engaged with God, or ignoring God?

Is God watching you because God delights in you or because God is watching you to catch your mistakes. Write about it here.

CHAPTER 9

Hell No!

This may be one of the most disputed of all the chapters. The image here is of a person who is suffering in what we call Hell. It is a place full of fire. It is total condemnation, total suffering, total and eternal separation from God. There are hundreds of ways to describe Hell.

Churches have invented many ways to go to Hell and rules to follow to get out of Hell. In some churches you can even pay money to keep out of Hell or get your loved ones out of Hell. Hell is the object of much speculation.

In the funny movie "My Blue Heaven," the uptight prosecutor (Joan Cusack) steps in front of the car driven by the FBI agent (Rick Moranis) when he is taking the bad guy (Steve Martin) a mafia hood New Yorker away from her jail. She steps in front of the car, refuses to move and swears at the men:

"Go to Hell! Just Go to Hell!" she yells. With that, the mafia thug jumps out of the car and says, "You gotta do better than that!"

For the guys in the movie, going to Hell is not much of a threat. However, in most churches, it is a great big bad threat.

At my church, having dipped our toes in the mystical journey of experiencing God's presence, love and even healing, we became more and more at odds with the idea of Hell.

How can God, who is supposed to be pure, forgiving love, ever consign his beloved creations to eternal damnation? It doesn't make any sense.

The congregation spent a couple of weekend retreats defining our belief system. We decided that Hell is actually a human construct, invented by men.

We had studied the New Testament and realized that when Jesus spoke of what we call Hell, he was referring to Gehenna. Gehenna was the garbage dump outside of the City of David's walls. Indeed, it was a place of darkness where the fire burning the garbage and trash never goes out and the worms that eat the garbage are always there, eating away. The worm never dies.

You might need to pursue this understanding more, but it is enough for me to say, from my own understanding and experience, that Hell is inconsistent with the nature of God. God's essence is love, pure love.

I discussed the process the church had gone through with my daughter Sarah and how it was difficult for me to understand why some of the folks wanted to cling to the idea of Hell. I thought it was a wonderful thing to be free of. Why would anyone want to believe they would or could go or be sent to Hell? Sarah with her uncanny insight into human behavior, said very clearly, "Oh, they want to believe in Hell because they want other people to go to Hell."

The concept of Hell is a very valuable weapon in the hands of the Church. It can be used as a threat and a way to control people. It can raise money and scare people. It is a tool of manipulation.

It is my strong opinion that it is an urban myth about God and is inconsistent with how God feels about us. Who wants to believe in or be close to a God who can send you to eternal suffering?

At this point people ask, if there is no Hell, what about Hitler? Doesn't he go to Hell? He certainly deserves to, that evil man.

I have come to consider another possibility. We have come to understand that each of us creates our own reality here on Earth. The choices we make create our lives, our realities. Jesus taught about this, too. We create the reality around us and we die with the reality we have chosen. Have we chosen God? We die with God. Have we not chosen God. We die without the reality of God in our lives. However, we are under grace and we are made of Spirit, in God's likeness. So, I believe we cross over into Heaven and we take our reality with us. If we die in anger and hate, we take that with us. We then continue our journey of healing in Heaven.

Again, we are like the ice cube when surrounded by heat, it melts. And we, in Heaven, are surrounded by the heat of God's love. Our hardness, anger and hate begin to melt and we have to work our way out of it. We are all souls in formation, in transformation. The goal is for us to become loving, to become love itself. We will continue the transformation process after we die.

I have come to this conclusion because I experience God's love. I experience God as love itself. I believe all our struggles are part of our transformation process. We get to choose to learn the lessons and be transformed by them, or to be defeated by them. If we are defeated, we can become angry, bitter, resentful and hateful. We are hurt and hurt people hurt people. Again, we choose. We all have work to do.

What do you imagine Hell is like?

_____

_____

_____

Is there someone you want to see go to Hell? Why?

_____

_____

_____

What would it be like to believe that Hell doesn't exist?

_____

_____

_____

If you are in transformation, what do you need to face in yourself and change?

_____

_____

_____

_____

What would be your healing goals?

_____

_____

_____

What would it take to reject the idea of Hell?

_____

_____

_____

What would it mean to you if Hell didn't exist? How would it change your life? How would it change your image of God?

_____

_____

_____

CHAPTER 10

The God Who Isn't There

An old friend, a lawyer, told me part of the story of his life. It wasn't a happy story even in the beginning. He was the oldest of 6 children. Birth control was not accepted by his parents' church so theirs was a big family. His parents were both disabled and lived on disability payments from the government and on the charity of the people of the church. It was a painful childhood. He prayed and prayed for God to intervene to help his family, and God never showed up.

Frankly, I don't know why.

The story improved as my friend, who was smart, earned a scholarship to a small, private college in our state. He went into the service and earned his law degree. He was a trial lawyer specializing in medical malpractice. He was and is very tough on the outside and has a true heart for those who have been unfairly hurt by powerful companies or institutions. His heart melts for the people he represents.

Now, he has done so well financially that he is semi-retired and working on his pet philanthropies. He and his wife help support a middle school in Cambodia that they visit regularly. They have added rooms to the school and provided computers.

They also are involved with the Wheelchair Warriors that raise money for wheelchairs to be distributed all over the world. He and his wife like to go participate in the distribution of the red wheelchairs chairs. They work with Rotary Clubs International who distribute them. They have traveled to South America, Nepal and Mexico.

Interestingly, though he doesn't have a relationship with God, he is doing the work of God all over the world. He is investing in people and their potential and alleviating suffering.

He is truly an inspiration to me.

And the question, why did God not show up for him, I don't know. I'm sure I don't know enough to even take a guess. It would be presumptuous of me.

This is what I do know, my friend, whether aware or not, lives in God's love. He moves in God's love and the energy of God lives in and through him. It is plain to see.

If you have experiences of God not showing up, share that here.

How did you feel about those times?

_____

_____

_____

I there something within you that is blocking God from loving you?

_____

_____

_____

SECTION II

Old Testament Images of God

The Old Testament images are very rich and plentiful. We will look as just a few. The distinction with the Old Testament is that it is the religious history of the Jewish people, or the Jewish Law, the Prophets and the Psalms, songs or worship and life. The Testament is very rich with history and wisdom and is important to the Christian religion and spirituality. It is the tradition that Jesus followed. Then Jesus changed everything.

The Old Testament is meant to represent the Covenant that God made with Abraham. It contains the history of the descendants of Abraham and the courageous adventures of the descendants and how they fulfilled their faith journeys of following God and following the law. It is also a record of how the Jewish people connected to God and how God connected with them.

The testament reveals to us now a record of the understanding the people of that time of the essence of the nature of God.

The stories also reveal an evolution of humankind's understanding of God.

God leads Abraham out of Ur toward the land He will give them. God frees the people from slavery in Egypt. God leads them to Canaan, the Promised Land, and establishes them as a great nation.

But this is not only a history of the Old Testament or of the Jewish people. It is a book of images of God and some of those images in this section are found there. We will look at just a few of them.

CHAPTER 11

Wrestle Mania

Jacob of the Old Testament, a terrible, lying, cheating and successful grandson of Abraham, son of Isaac, has cheated his older brother Esau out of his birthright. They have been estranged for years. Each of them has greatly prospered in livestock, goods, wives, children and servants. Jacob decides it is time for him to go and be reconciled to his brother. They live a nomadic life, following their livestock needs, and Jacob leads his family on the long journey to reconciliation. He is totally scared that his brother will take out his wrath on Jacob and all who are associated with him. They come to the river Jabbok on the last leg of the journey. Jacob sends everyone over the river and he stays the night alone. He is deathly afraid.

A "man" appears and starts to wrestle with Jacob. Some versions refer to the man as an angel. They wrestle all night long. By daybreak the man sees that he cannot defeat Jacob and stops the fight. Jacob says he refuses to stop until he receives the man's blessing. The man asks his name, Jacob replies "Jacob". The man says that his name will no longer be Jacob but "Israel" because he has wrestled with both God and man and has overcome. The man, the angel, however, touches Jacob Israel's hip and wounds him. He will limp for the rest of his life as a reminder of the event.

Jacob names the place Peniel which means "I have seen God face to face and, yet, my life was spared."

This is one of my favorite Old Testament stories. It is certainly metaphorical for our lives. We all have struggles in life: difficult relationships, poverty, grueling work, illness, deaths of loved ones. I can easily think that each of us is like Jacob, wrestling with great difficulties, Also, we wrestle with emotions: fear, anger, depression, shyness, inferiority, mental illness, addiction. And we keep wrestling. If we persevere, we can receive the blessing that comes after the struggle, though we will be marred by the fight.

In terms of the Image of God, we see that, in these ancient Biblical times God appears as a man. The image of God as a man is well represented in the story of Abraham and Sarah. God appears as 3 men to Abraham. Then, later, two of them are called angels and they depart for Sodom and Gomorrah.

With Jacob, it is a man who wrestles with Jacob. Many people refer to the man as an angel. Gaugin, the famous French artist created a painting of Jacob wrestling an angel. Then, after Jacob receives the blessing he declares, "I have seen God face to face."" The man is, in fact, God Himself.

In our transforming, growing process, it is helpful to change our view of our struggles, as a process that strengthens us. They do not weaken us.

Name some events in your life that have been struggles. Have you overcome? Or been defeated?

_____

_____

_____

Were there times, when the wrestling was over, that you could see and name the blessing?

_____

_____

_____

CHAPTER 12

Wildfire: The Burning Bush

The story of Moses begins in the book of Exodus. Moses is in charge of his father-in-law's sheep and follows them to the mountain named Horeb, also known as the mountain of God. Exodus 3 tells us that an angel of the Lord appeared as flames in a bush, but the bush was not burned up. Moses approaches to see what on Earth is happening. When he gets close enough, the scripture tells us that God saw him approach and ordered him to remove his shoes, since this is a holy place. Where God is, is holy. Then God announces himself as God. Moses hides his face so as not to look at God. Rumors have been swirling for generations that, if you look at God, you will die. As we saw in the last image, Jacob was astounded that he had seen God face to face and didn't die. But the rumor is still flourishing.

God commissions Moses to go to Egypt and bring his people, the Israelites, out of Egypt. And the rest is history, we could say.

The purpose here is to examine the images of God represented in this story and to see how they might be relevant to us in our time.

First it is an angel that appears in flames, as fire in a bush. We see the Burning Bush as being God. What I like about this image is that the presentation of God as a man has changed. In Genesis the stories of God describe him as a man, or an angel that looks like a man. Now God is seen as fire. He also gives his name, "I AM that I AM." This name has been a puzzlement to me. Many scholars love this descriptive name. Jews are not supposed to even write God's name. But now, I have finally discerned that this name, at least for me, means, "I am Being Itself." Or "I am Life Force." It becomes a powerful, active name, not contained in human form but beyond human form. This image shakes things up quite a bit.

How does this image relate to your experience?

Have you encountered God in an unusual place, in an unusual Presence?

_____

_____

_____

Has God addressed you personally? Asked you to do something?

_____

_____

_____

What possibilities does this image present to your understanding?

_____

_____

_____

Has God addressed you personally? Asked you to do something?

CHAPTER 13

Lost at Sea

In this image of God, I am trying to capture the idea of God as the Sea of Forgetfulness. The image is referring to the pronouncement of Micah 7:19:

> "You will again have compassion on us,
> You will tread our sins underfoot
> And hurl all our iniquities
> Into the depths of the sea."

In other words, God throws all our sins, faults, mistakes into the Sea of Forgetfulness and remembers them no more. What a relief!

In the painting we see God's profile, which represents the mind of God, and his long hair forms into waves representing the sea. Notice, too, that God's moustache, lips, and beard represent the profile of a Woman. In this image I unconsciously painted God as both masculine and feminine. I didn't even realize it until I projected the picture on the screen during a sermon at church. A woman came running up to me after church to ask if I had included the feminine image of God on purpose. I had to find the original to see for myself. Sure enough, I had painted God as both masculine and feminine.

This image actually represents the belief that God forgets our mistakes. The belief that God not only forgives our mistakes but totally forgets them could have a profound effect on our relationship with God. As my friend, Ginny said, "God walks around with his little black book, watching us and making note of all of our mistakes, sins."

What if God really forgets?

There was a woman who started listening to God during prayer time. It's true that we can talk to God and hear a response. Many Christians are unaware of and uninformed of this spiritual practice. She was so excited that she was listening to the Spirit and beginning to hear God speak. She was part of the Charismatic Renewal that emphasizes and teaches this kind of prayer. Her excitement bubbled over at church one day and she told her Priest, "I'm learning how to listen to God when I pray."

After a moment the Priest said to her, "Next time you are praying, ask God what the sin was that a young seminarian committed when he was studying to be a Priest,"

She said, "Ok, I will."

The next time he saw her he asked if she had asked God his question. "Oh, yes," she replied.

Shame-faced, the Priest, looking at his feet, asked, "What did he say?" "Oh," she exclaimed, "He said that He forgot!"

Whew! The Priest was so relieved!

Some churches and religions have turned our relationship with God into a horrible abusive situation where we are burdened with guilt and shame, feeling we can't measure up to God's standards and requirements.

This is why forgiveness is so important. It is vital to our lives with God and to our lives in general. We need to ask for forgiveness from God and others and, most of all, learn to forgive ourselves. Cast our cares into the Sea of Forgetfulness.

How would your life with God change if God wants us to grow and live guilt free? It would be a joyful experience if God doesn't remember any of our mistakes, or slip-ups or our accidents.

Remember a specific mistake you made that still haunts you. How would your life be different if God had completely forgiven you and you had forgiven yourself? What if God threw it into the Sea of Forgetfulness?

SECTION III

New Testament Images of God

In the New Testament God appears to humankind as Jesus. He is full of the energy and essence of God. People respond to the power of his presence. He is God with skin on.

Jesus teaches with such authority like the people have never seen or experienced. He heals thousands of people during a sermon. He casts out demons and even raises the dead. He is miraculous. And he teaches. Jesus was a master of telling stories and his stories reveal what God is like. He uses simple descriptions of God using common, ordinary stories of life. God is like a woman who lost a coin, a hen with her chicks, a man who lost his son.

Then the New Testament writers describe God in adjectives and attributes. It is what we call a word image. See if you can create images of God through their word images. We will take a look at a few images to see how Jesus describes God and God's relationship to us.

CHAPTER 14

The Lost Coin

There once was a woman who had 10 silver coins. One day she realized that one was gone. It was lost! She was so distraught that she began to tear the house apart looking for the lost coin. She swept, she dusted, she rearranged everything. Suddenly there it was, under her favorite winged-backed chair. What a relief! What a joy! She was so excited she called all her neighbors together for a party. They all celebrated with her because part of her good fortune, her treasure, had been lost and now it was found.

And what a party it was!

This story, told by Jesus and recorded in Luke 15. It is one of three stories: Parable of the Lost Sheep, the Lost Coin and the Lost Son. I have illustrated two of the stories. The stories illustrate God as the Good Shepherd, the Woman, and the Father. That makes the story of the Lost Coin more significant.

These stories are told by Jesus and reveal that he is comfortable portraying God as both male and female. In fact, it seems to me that the story of the Coin is set in the middle of the three stories so that it doesn't get lost. In that way the image of God the Woman is emphasized.

However, the gist of the story is that when God loses something that is a treasure to Her, she will do anything She can to find it.

First the sheep is lost. God the Shepherd searches and hunts until He finds the missing sheep. Then God the Woman loses her treasure and searches, cleans and hunts until She finds it.

Then God the Father watches until His lost son returns home to Him.

The stories have three similarities, God is in human form, male and female. A treasured object or person is lost, God searches or waits until the object/person is found, a big celebration begins because that which was lost to God has been found!

The inference here is that God parties when He/She finds what is lost! God rejoices when a person who is lost to God returns to God.

If you are distant from God, relate how this story relates to you?

_____

_____

_____

Are you God's Treasure?

_____

_____

_____

Are you lost or found?

_____

_____

_____

Write your reflections.

_____

_____

_____

If you are distant from God, relate how this story relates to you?

CHAPTER 15

Hen and Chicks

A photographer took his trusty camera down to the nearby pond to hopefully catch a glimpse of the local beavers at work. He didn't see any of his target subjects but found something far more unusual. A couple of geese were there escorting their 6 goslings. The photographer snapped a few shots and vowed to return the next night. Again, he was disappointed to not locate the beavers but came across the geese couple again. Only, this time, the geese had 15 babies in tow. After a couple more sessions of photography, the geese were herding a group of 25 geese. When the babies were small enough, the mama could gather them together to protect them under her wings. As the babies grew, they were too large to fit under the mama. She and her mate would gather them into a tight bunch and guard them from harm.

Fascinated by this discovery, the photographer studied the lives of geese. He learned that this gathering of babies is a result of some geese being better mothers than others. It seems that those who would not be good at mothering, gave up their babies to the super momma. The phenomenon is called a "group brood." What a beautiful occurrence of intentional nurturing, intentional mothering in nature.

The people of Jesus's day were well acquainted with the ways of chickens and geese. They had probably been well acquainted with this super-mothering. And then, in Mathew 23 Jesus described God as a hen with her chicks. It was a rather outlandish image of God. It is a very dynamic image of God as the ultimate nurturer. However, it is outlandish for another reason, a hen with her chick is a feminine image of God. This would shock the conscious of the Jews of Jesus 's day.

The Jews of Jesus's era were Orthodox. They held God in such high esteem that they were not allowed to write or speak God's name. That tradition holds forth today. My orthodox Jewish friends on Face Book write a shortened form of God's name, even on Face Book entries. There were prescribed ways that Jews thought about God and Jesus was shaking up the rules. Jesus introduced the femininity of God.

Psalm 91 contains a similar image of God that every person of Jesus's era would have been familiar with. It goes like this:

> He who dwells in the shelter of the Most High
> Will abide in the shadow of the Almighty.
> I will say to the Lord, "My refuge and my fortress

My God in whom I trust!"
For it is He who delivers you from the snare of the trapper,
And from the deadly pestilence.
He will cover you with His pinions,
And under His wings you may seek refuge.
His faithfulness is a shield and bulwark.

While this passage is chock full of vivid images of God, we are considering how masculine the image is of the mothering bird protecting her chicks. This Old Testament image of God is a feminine image of God and Jesus reintroduces the feminine image of God.

One night, several months after my husband had passed away, I was hungering for one of my favorite dishes at a local restaurant. I decided to go out by myself. The tables are always full at O'Neill's Grille, so I signed in and sat at the bar to enjoy a glass of white wine while waiting. There was an older couple sitting next to me so we began to visit. I learned that the man, in his mid-70s, was a retired banker who had spent years commuting from his home in the Kansas City area to his job in New York City. But then he began talking about his true joy and passion.

It seems he was at a men's retreat in his church and a speaker was presenting about some of the struggles of poor families in the area. At the end of the talk, someone from the audience piped up, saying, "What are we going to do about it?"

That was the beginning of a reading program that the group started to address the needs of those who were underserved by the educational system. This man was the head of the organization. The program grew to 3,000 participants. The group bought an old school, bought buses, and taught children to read in the summers.

It was amazing watching this man's face. As happens to all of us, the skin on the man's face had grown soft and was falling in gentle folds and wrinkles. But when he talked about the school, his face lit up, his smile defeated the wrinkles, and I could see the presence of God in his soul.

His wife sat there, taking it all in, so I asked how she was involved. She liked to work behind the scenes. She painted classrooms and generally helped in the production.

I told them I was working on this book about God and could I use their story. And, what would they like to see in the book? Immediately, without hesitation, the woman said, "I want to see pictures of the feminine God; I want to see Mother God!"

She like many women I know, in church, in Seminary, in the world long to be included in the image of God, to see their hearts and souls reflected in the Divine.

They invited me to sit there and eat with them. We continued talking about the One we love most., God.

It was no small thing that Jesus described God a mother hen with her chicks. Many hearts are yearning to see our Divine Mother.

Was your mother a warm nurturing woman?

Or was your mother cold, remote, removed, not nurturing? Take a few minutes to describe your mother and your relationship.

Would seeing, being with a mothering God be helpful or hurtful?

Our first experience of God can be reflected in our relationships with our mother and father. What would feel the most comforting to you?

CHAPTER 16

The Lost Child

It is so devastating to lose a child whether to drugs, through estrangement, fights, or disagreements. Pride and arrogance can separate parents from children.

I have listened to anguished parents share their pain when a child leaves home and becomes seduced into or outright chooses a life of drugs and abandoned their family's values and hopes and dreams for those children.

I know a family who, when their son continued to choose to use drugs, they packed up a duffle bag of his things and told him to leave until he was finished with the drug lifestyle. He was 18 at the time. He never returned home but did give up his addiction and reestablished his relationship with his parents. This is called "tough love" in our day.

I think of the years of agony the parents went through, loving their son, longing for him to fix his life, yearning for the life they had with him and fearful of the danger that surrounded him. They had decided to let him go to figure out his life, his path without them.

The story in Luke 15 is about a father who lets his son go to find himself. However, it's not "tough love" because the son asks for his inheritance. The father gives it to him. Off he goes to create his life. He has many friends who help him spend all his money. When the money is gone, the friends go with it.

The son finds himself penniless and has no food or means of support. He finally finds a job minding pigs. He is so hungry even the pig food looks good to him. But no one even gives him that much.

He remembers that his father's lowliest servants have food even food to spare. He is humbled and decides to return home to his father and beg for a job as a servant since he has disgraced himself. He returns home. His father has been watching for him. He has gone out to watch for him every day that he is gone. One day the father sees him coming home, even when he is still far off.

With incredible joy the father runs to meet his son. The son humbles himself and begs forgiveness and pleads for a job. The father sends for a new, best robe for his son. He places a ring on his finger and calls for the fattened calf to be slaughtered for a grand party. He invites all the neighbors and kin folk to come and celebrate for his beloved son, who was lost, has come home.

Of course, as Jesus tells this story, he reveals God who plays the father, and the son who represents each of us who have not yet come home to God.

You might wonder if this is just an old story without much meaning for us today. As I previously revealed there are still families where the children get lost and the parents grieve the loss and wait for them to find their way home.

However, I have a modern-day story that shows how God seeks us and wants us to return to friendship with Her/Him. This is one of my favorite stories of all time. It happened to my friend, Ellen. It is so much a part of who she is that I think it is not as amazing to her as it is to me!

Ellen moved to my little town when we were in 6th grade. She was the cousin of my sister's best friend so I felt I had to welcome her. We became Besties from then on. In our high school years, we both began a serious search for God. We went to different churches but together we visited a couple of other churches. God was a frequent topic of conversation for us.

We went our separate ways during college. I was away for my junior year living and studying in France when Ellen wrote that she had found God when she dedicated her life to Jesus. I was soon to follow in her footsteps. Finding God and God's incredible love was life altering! We have continued our God path ever since. We have been friends now for 62 years. This is one of her stories.

When in college in Columbia, Missouri, Ellen worked for a couple who ran a little café called the Busy Bee. Then, after college Ellen went on her way. Fast forward about 20 years. One day Ellen gets an impression from God that she has to find Kathryn Ann, the woman she worked for at the café. Of course, Ellen had not seen Kathryn Ann for about 20 years and didn't know where to start looking. The internet was fairly new so her brother helped her search for Kathryn Ann. He found nothing. The pressure of the impression on her heart persisted. She just had to find Kathryn Ann!

Ellen tried everything she could to find her friend. Finally, Ellen found Kathryn Ann's husband. They had been divorced for a few years and had lost touch. However, the last he had heard, she was waiting tables in Grandview, a city just south of Kansas City. Ellen had a clue at last!

Ellen made jewelry and had a jewelry business. One day she had to go to a trade show in Kansas City so she decided to stop in Grandview to take a stab at finding Kathryn Ann. She thought Grandview was just a spot in the road. Lo and behold, when she got to Grandview there were three exists for the town. The population was almost 25,000 people. It was not just a spot in the road. She saw a building that looked like a hotel with a restaurant on the main floor. That is where she would start her search.

As Ellen drove up to the building, she saw that the restaurant was closed. Ratz! What to do? She decided to charge on with the search since she was there. She went in to the hotel front desk and made up a story.

She said, "I have a friend who was waiting tables here and I wonder if you know anything about her. Her name is Kathryn Ann."

To that the desk clerk replied, "Oh, Kathy? She's in the back! I'll go get her!" (Take a moment to be amazed!)

Out comes Kathryn Ann and, in amazement says, "Ellen, what are you doing here:"

Ellen asks if there is a private place they can talk. They go sit in the corner of the lobby and Ellen asks, "Is there some reason God would send me to find you?"

Kathryn Ann bursts into tears and tells Ellen that she had been so close to God before but had fallen in with a group of friends that didn't really want to be with God and she was pulling away herself.

God had sent Ellen into the unknown to find Kathryn Ann and to bring her home.

The next time I saw Ellen she was at a women's retreat at a church and Kathryn Ann was with her, her loving relationship with God restored!

God still searches or waits or sends someone to find us and bring us home. Do you need to be found, or retrieved? Write about your experience.

_____

_____

_____

CHAPTER 17

The Daddy

While teaching French and being a school counselor just out of graduate school, I found my job in a tiny school in a tiny rural town just north of the bootheel in Missouri. I loved the town and I loved the school. But most of all, I loved my students. I picked up a precious way the students talked about their fathers. One boy in particular talked about his father in a most affectionate way. He referred to his father as "my Daddy." My Daddy said this, or my Daddy did that. It was a most endearing way that he spoke about his father. It was charming, kind of Southern and very unfamiliar to me.

I didn't have a daddy. I had a father. And that's what we called him, Father. My father was a very quiet, driven, intense man. He was never given to small talk. He lectured and he lectured us. He had grown up, as had my mother, in the depression. My father left high school at 15 because he had been accepted in- to college. He left college at 18 to attend medical school at Washington University in St. Louis, Missouri. Money was tight and he tried to get through his education in record time so as not to use more of his father's money. His father was a small- town medical doctor, a general practitioner, as they were called. My father went on to become a general surgeon. I can only now imagine how stressed out he must have been.

We called him "Father."

I was in 6th grade talking on the phone with my best friend, Ellen, when I changed the formal term "Father" inadvertently. My oldest sister had finished her first year at college and came home all superior and putting on airs. I was making fun of her to my friend.

"Lucia, (my sister) is now abbreviating all her words," I complained. "She calls the Library, the Libe." I went on.

"Soon she'll be calling Mother, Muth and Father, Fath!." I was incensed.

Unbeknownst to me, the whole family was just in the other room finishing up their supper, listening to my conversation. Apparently, they liked my new abbreviations. From then on, we called our mother, 'Muth, and our father "Fath."

It was less formal but nowhere near the endearing term "My Daddy," or even Daddy or Dad.

Our relationship with God often reflects our early relationships with our parents. My experience dictated a formal, distant connection. That's pretty much how I related to God as well, distant, formal.

Then Jesus, much to my surprise, to the surprise and amazement of his compatriots and everyone ever since he walked the Earth, called God "Abba" which means "Daddy."

Daddies come in all shapes, sizes and colors. Some people are lucky enough to relate warmly to their Daddies, others aren't. However, if we can confront and change our image of Daddy God to reflect the loving, supportive, encouraging One that Daddy God truly is, how life would change!

Reflect on your relationship with your father and how that relationship has affected your relationship to God.

Were you close to your dad? Distant?

Some of us don't know our fathers at all. If that's true for you, how has that affected your relationship to God?

Can you imagine cuddling up with God to talk? Try to imagine that right now.

Curl up on the sofa or in your favorite comfy chair, wrap up in a blanket and imagine. Let the tender love of God enfold you. Your Daddy is here.

It's mind blowing! Jesus is describing his relationship with God using this warm, intimate, endearing term, Daddy. Jesus was as close and open with God as some people are with their earthly fathers. This changes everything.

My doctor's nurse, Joyce, shared with me that she doesn't think about God much. She is a church goer and a believer and she was a daddy's girl. He had passed away and she missed him terribly. However, because of her closeness with "her daddy," she was no longer afraid of death because she knew he was waiting for her there on the other side. No ifs, ands or buts. She knew this truth with no doubt. I felt comforted just hearing her belief.

God as Daddy, warm, nurturing, fun and loving. What a wonderful way to experience God.

CHAPTER 18

Jesus the Feminist

A disgraced one doesn't come to the well
In the morning
Among friends
And greetings
She comes alone
At noon
"Give me a drink," he said.
"Jews don't talk to Samaritans," her retort.
"Bring your husband; we will talk."
"No husband."
"Indeed, 5 husbands and now, with a man
Not married."
"How did you know?"
"I am He
For whom you wait."
"Living water, I give
No more thirst
No more shame."
The first evangelist she became.
Bringing the others to hope
To Life
To living water
To Jesus
Ahhh, that woman,
The disgraced.

Dare I say that this is one of my very favorite Jesus stories? Jesus sees the woman's heart and offers her the gift of living water. Living water is different from well water, like is found in Jacob's well. It is different from pond water or lake water. It is from a stream of water that is fresh and cleansing and renewing. I remember hearing that if there is a dead animal in a stream, a mile away, downstream, the water will be cleansed enough to drink. God's living water is fresh and cleansing.

Jesus is offering her a life in the Spirit that renews what is damaged, dead, disgraced in her. They have a theological discussion about the historically correct location for worship of the Most High. Jesus reveals that the time is coming in which people will worship God anywhere. God is Spirit and people will worship God in Spirit and truth. This is huge!

We see her transformation throughout the story. She is alone, defiled, rejected, outcast. Jesus sees her heart and she is transformed by the energy and presence of God within him. She is renewed, enlivened and empowered. She becomes an evangelist. Throwing off her shame, she runs to get the townspeople and brings them to Jesus. He stays in the village for two days, in a Samaritan town for two days and many become believers.

The rules for relating with women in Jesus's day were very strict. In public, men didn't relate to women very much or openly. I can imagine the street scenes were very much as the street scenes in the Middle East minus the cars, the skyscrapers, motorcycles and even bicycles. I read a book describing a woman's life in Saudi Arabi. She had to cover herself up with a burqa so no men could see her outside of her home. If she went in public, she always had to be escorted by her husband or a male relative.

Even in this modern day, in the Middle East, women are seen as second-class citizens. They are fighting for the freedoms that we in the West enjoy. The struggle continues.

I'm not sure that ancient Israel was this restrictive but, I do know that, when Jesus engaged in open conversation with the woman at the well, he was breaking some serious taboos. This showcases the story in stark contrast to the norms of the day.

Jesus shows that women are worthy, are loved, are gifted by God to present the transforming Presence of God in the world. God heals women of physical wounds, psychological wounds, social wounds and sends them into the world to heal the world.

Even in this day, in some Christian communities, women are denied the ability to minister to men or in congregations in general. They are not allowed to lead the church or to preach to the congregation. I was part of a congregation connected to a denomination like that. We went against the rules. We had four ordained women on staff and our local association tried to kick us out of the denomination. A meeting was held and we were allowed to stay "in" by 4 votes. In our congregation we didn't take the Bible literally, but we took it seriously. The story of the Woman at the Well caused us to change our stance on women and women in ministry. Jesus's message is challenging and transforming. Perhaps this story should be reviewed to get to the heart of Jesus's message, God's message. Women are called to minister in the world. They are called to be part of the next incarnation of God in humankind, just as men are.

Women are called to minister God's Presence in the world today. God's Presence is transformational.

Have you experienced prejudice or bigotry or misogyny? Have you been devalued because of who you are, your skin color, your gender, your socioeconomic status, your education?

Write how that felt to you.

_____

_____

_____

How would life be different if you were equal and equally valued? If your gifts were deemed valued in your community? Write about these things.

_____

_____

_____

_____

_____

I AM THAT I AM

LOVE
JOY
PEACE
PATIENCE
KINDNESS
FAITHFULNESS
GOODNESS
GENTLENESS
SELF-CONTROL
Galatians 5:22-23

CHAPTER 19

Word Image

Fruit of the Spirit

"For the fruits of the Spirit are

Love,

    joy,

        peace,

            patience,

                kindness,

                    goodness,

                        faithfulness

                            gentleness

                              and self-control."

Galatians 5:22-23

This is a very well-known scripture for Christians. It is from a letter from the Apostle Paul to the church at Galatia. He is encouraging the people to let the Holy Spirit within them produce aspects of personality that were found in Jesus. They are descriptors of Jesus and also of God. In effect, this scripture is a word picture of God.

The word picture is about Jesus, the Holy Spirit and God. Jesus, in whom the Spirit dwelt and created vibrant energy. The Spirit within him reflected the image and power of God. This is the work of the Holy Spirit which is the embodied energy of God that lives in all of us. Many people are totally unaware of the Presence of God within.

In essence these words describe God. To experience God is to experience love, joy, peace, patience, kindness, goodness, faithfulness, gentleness and self-control.

Sit with this word image of God and let these attributes of God sink into your heart. God loves you.

Write about what you discover.

_____

_____

_____

_____

_____

_____

The Forgotten Image

In Genesis the story about God presents us with a vital image of God. Half of that image has been forgotten and the consequences for the human race and civilization have been disastrous. I can see why some of the confusion has occurred, and for the sake of our evolving awareness, the confusion must be addressed. The forgotten image must be resurrected and affirmed.

The confusion begins in the beginning when the writer of Genesis records two creation stories. The stories concern the creation of man and woman, Adam and Eve. The first story portrays God creating humans in God's image, male and female God created them. This is a story of the co-equals of the human race. The female image of God is the forgotten image.

The second creation story suggests that Eve was created from Adam's rib. Being created from the side of Adam, the writer describes Eve as a helper of Adam. This is not a story of equality, at least in how many people interpret the story.

In the movie *Noah*, starring Russel Crowe as Noah, Noah is sitting at a campfire with his family and is telling the story of creation. Just watching him share the oral tradition story helps show the passing down of the Jewish God tradition. The story, at that stage, is not read from a book or a scroll but is a story told from memory. It is an oral tradition. Was it word for word? Or was it stories remembered and shared? This image from the movie made a great impact on me.

I believe the essence of the tradition is preserved as scriptures of the Old Testament, the Pentateuch and Law of the Jewish religion. And it began as oral tradition, campfire stories.

The forgotten image of God, God as Female, Mother God, the Sacred Feminine is vital to express, explain and uphold, to continue to advance the equality of women and to elevate the consciousness of humankind.

As of this writing, women in Iran are protesting the wearing of the hijab. It is a scarf that is required by the government for the women to cover their hair. A woman, Mahsa, was wearing one but incorrectly according to the Morality Police in Iran. They arrested her and she died in prison. Now it is the longest lasting protest against the strict Muslim government. The hijab is the symbol of men ruling over women. Women are the second-class citizens, the helpers of men.

In Afghanistan, at this writing, the British Broadcasting Company published an article about a missing woman. Afghanistan was on its way to becoming a free, independent country when the Taliban took over. Alia Azizi was in charge of the local prison. She had to quit her job when the Taliban took charge. A group of educated activists reported, when they asked the Taliban if women were going to keep their rights and be able to go to school and work, the leaders said no. They said there would be no women working in the Taliban government. Alia was asked to return to work at the prison. She did. Then she disappeared. Her family has not heard from her for 10 months. Many women have disappeared because women are deemed second class. Women are deemed unimportant.

We must restore the forgotten image. The Sacred Feminine is an equal part of God and women are an equal part of humankind. The feminine must be restored to equality.

CHAPTER 20

You Look Just Like Her

She Looks Just Like You

Ken and I have two daughters, Lucia and Sarah. When they were young it was clear that our eldest looked like Ken. She had the same jaw line and was petite like Ken's mom. However, she had blue eyes, blond hair and rosy cheeks, just like me.

Everyone else would ask, "Who does Sarah, the youngest, look like?" It wasn't clear except that she was tall like Ken and had dark hair and green eyes, like him.

When I was contemplating the feminine aspect of God, I needed to hear directly from God what the truth was about Her. I had been introduced to a relationship with God by a boyfriend. Besides following Jesus, he was a staunch believer in the man being the head of the household and the head of the relationship. It was a traditional way to see relationships by more fundamentalist believers. It was very damaging to me, to my self-esteem. Fortunately, we ended our relationship and I married Ken, who believed in total equality in our marriage. It took me years to heal from the damage that patriarchal system did to my soul.

Then I began exploring the feminine face of God. When we are looking at God through our wounded hearts, we need healing. I wanted to know the truth about God and the equality of the male and female. I asked God to show me who She is.

One night, as I was tucking Sarah in to bed and saying goodnight, an amazing thing happened. The bedside lamp was on and the way the light fell on her face, I realized that she looked just like me. For the first time I realized that Sarah looked just like me. I had never seen that before. I saw that she was my mirror image. As I gazed at her I heard God speak to me in that still small voice….

"Just as she looks like you, so you look like me!"

The message struck me at the very core of my being. God looked like me and I looked like Her. God was just as feminine as I was. God is just as much feminine as masculine, just as much Mother, as Father, just as much Sister as Brother, just as much Wife as Husband. I was floored! Then, I was at peace. God brought healing in a place where I had been very deeply wounded.

So many women are abused in the name of patriarchal religion, Christianity included. Discovering the feminine nature of God can be very confrontive to our personal beliefs and the patriarchal system. It is vital to affirm the truth about the feminine aspect of the Holy Being. Women need to understand that they carry the Divine likeness in their essence. They represent the Holy Presence of God on the Earth in equal fashion to men.

The people of the world need healing of the Divine Feminine. Until then, the world cannot be healed.

How do you feel about the Divine Feminine?

_____

_____

_____

If God was like a mother to you, would that be good or bad, healing or hurtful? Explain.

_____

_____

_____

If God was a loving Mother to you, a Holy Mother, how would that change your life and your relationship to God?

_____

_____

_____

_____

_____

_____

_____

_____

CHAPTER 21

Breakfast God

I was in therapy for several years. Therapy was lauded as one of the newer paths for emotional healing and our church leadership encouraged people to get therapy. Some people in the church were really upset thinking that only prayer and God could fix everything. I was aware of my personal pain and sought healing wherever I could. God and I went into therapy together. I sought God in all the new aspects of my life, my wounds and my healing. It was and still is an amazing journey.

I muse over the attitude that medicine, therapy, psychology are not tools of God. I affirm that God not only uses these tools but also helped people discover the methods and medicines to heal. I believe that God is in all wonderful methods of healing. We can rejoice and jump in there to deal with trauma, abandonment, abuse and addictions. We can be healed! Healing prayer is also dynamic and helpful and fascinating. But this is not the focus of this image of God.

While I was in therapy, I was dealing with my mother wounds when this wonderful vision came to me. Visions are simply pictures that pop into one's head and serve as a message from the Spirit. One can learn to tune into the mind where this communication takes place.

My mother could be a lot of fun and was full of excitement and adventure. She took me and my friends to frozen ponds to skate on in the Winter. She was our Girl Scout leader and took us camping in the Summer and Fall. And she wasn't the warm, cuddly and nurturing type. She was also consumed with care for my older sister who dealt with health issues. My other sister and I were on our own in many ways.

My mother also didn't like to cook. She pretty much hated it. She loved to read cookbooks all afternoon and then cook the same old things for dinner. I still can't look at a cubed steak at the store and not remember the shoe leather consistency of my mother's cooking method. She could fix a fabulous holiday meal and excellent Saturday night hamburger. There was always enough for any last moment visitors. However, the variety was scant.

My friend since Kindergarten, Ginny, had me over for dinner once in the 4th grade. Her mother had made home-made chicken and noodles. I apparently expressed over and over again my amazement that she had made the noodles herself. It seems the story of my appreciation became a family story for them. I still enjoy the variety of foods available everywhere!

One day, during a therapy session this amazing picture came to me. All these issues merged into a single healing image. It was God in an apron, fixing me breakfast. She was a large black older woman like my spiritual mother, Miss Eva Saunders. She was warm and soft and singing to me. She was comforting and nurturing. She filled my heart with love.

Years later a book was published and then a movie was made called *The Shack* by William Paul Young. There God was, described then portrayed as a large black woman, cooking to nurture her loved ones. We are all her loved ones. This had been my vision. This is Breakfast God!

Sit and ponder this image.

Does it speak to you?

_____

_____

_____

Does it comfort you?

_____

_____

_____

Write about your reaction to this image.

_____

_____

_____

If God was a warm, nurturing Mom to you, what would she look like?

_____

_____

_____

CHAPTER 22

Clair of Assisi

Chris, a friend from Integral Christian Network, shared her spiritual journey with me. It seems that her mother was a very harsh, strict woman of German descent. She did not have a warm nurturing mother growing up. Hers is another example of how our relationship with our parents can hinder or help our relationship with God. If our first impression of God is who our parents are to us, then it's no wonder we would have trouble wanting to relate to God.

Years ago, I was in a small group and met a couple who were friends of a group member. The couple seemed to be struggling with life and had seemingly come from a difficult background with not much nurturing. They had a baby boy and it was time for him to have a bottle. He was about 7 months old. The mom gave him the bottle and lay him down on the floor. She explained that he didn't like being held even when he had his bottle. Something in my heart clutched and I found myself fearing for his future. If he couldn't take in nurturing at 7 months, how was he going to take in love and nurture as he got older? We never saw them again but I have often wondered about him.

As we grow up, we learn how to give and receive love, if we are lucky. As a school counselor for 6 years and a pastor for almost 30, I find that many of us have trouble taking in love. Our parents did the best they could at loving us and we learned from them. They could only give love the way they received love. Sometimes that was very successful sometimes it was not. Most of us have mother and father wounds, places in our soul that lack the love we need. As we grow and consciously pursue our healing journey we take in mothering and fathering energy from people around us. We can continue healing our souls.

The friend I mentioned chose Claire of Assisi as her role model and as her spiritual teacher. To learn about her helped heal the mother wound inside of her. Such holy saints serve as spirit guides on our journey. It is another way of experiencing the Sacred Feminine.

How would you approach connecting with the Sacred Feminine, Mother God?

_____

_____

_____

Are there any special women in your life or in your memory that would help heal the mother wound within you?

_____

_____

_____

Who would that person be and what would she look like?

_____

_____

_____

CHAPTER 23

Mary, Mother of God

Maria was my roommate in graduate school. She was from Brazil. She grew up on a farm in northern Brazil with 14 brothers and sisters. The girls watched the sheep while the boys worked the fields. She shared that, while she watched the sheep, she would lean against a tree, gazing at the horizon. She often wondered what was on the horizon. In school, she passed the university test and went to college. Then as her brothers and sisters passed the test, she helped them get started. Maria applied for an advanced teacher program at University of Missouri, came to America and we became roommates and friends. She married an American and their daughter became a doctor and participated in an advanced program at Harvard University. It is the stuff that dreams are made of.

Maria, like a lot of Brazilians, is Roman Catholic. She shares that Mother Mary, Jesus's mother, was always who she was close to and who was her guide.

I understand that it was the people of the Roman Catholic church that adored Mary and the leaders (the men of the church) had to adopt what became the Cult of Mary. Because of the demand of the people, Mary became official.

The Catholics were lucky in that they became aware of the need to connect with the Sacred Feminine.

Through the Lily Endowment, I received a clergy-renewal grant to take a 4 months sabbatical. I was to do what made my heart sing! It was a wonderful experience!

My husband and I went to France so I could "paint in southern France just like Van Gogh." We started in Paris and saw many things, first of all being Versailles, palace of King Louis XIV. It was absolutely gorgeous and packed with people from all over the world.

I had bought an iPad 2 so I could take pictures. It was brand new to the market, the first to take pictures. I heard other tourists whispering behind my back..." It's an iPad 2." It was great to be the cool kid with the newest digital toy.

As we toured Versailles, Ken got angrier and angrier. I finally asked what was bothering him. He said that no man deserved such opulence. A quizzical reaction, I thought.

Then we went to Lourdes to visit the shrine. Ken wasn't interested so I went alone. It was my turn to be angry!

I had read the story. A poor shepherd girl (like Maria?) had seen a vision of a woman from Heaven. The woman from Heaven touched a stone and water came flowing out. It created a stream that is still there. It is said that the water could heal people.

There is a beautiful church there to commemorate the miracle. On the ceiling of the church is a mosaic of the Virgin Mary…stunning. I stepped into the church in time to catch the end of Mass. That's when I started to steam! At the altar were two priests dressed in gorgeous brocade robes and one little nun in a very plain gray habit. Furious! Livid! How had they missed the message???

The message had come to a young girl from a woman from Heaven. And now the men were in charge of it all. It seems to me that many churches continue to miss the message. Women and girls are sacred.

Do you see women as second-class citizens or as sacred, carrying the image of God?

_____

_____

_____

How has the church influenced you understanding of women?

_____

_____

_____

What other influences have affected your understanding of women in society.

_____

_____

_____

How did your mother influence your understanding of women and their position in your home and your community?

_____

_____

_____

CHAPTER 24

Dreamer Creator

With a cloud as her pillow
And Earth at her feet,
Ursa Major pulls a blanket of stars
Over her while she sleeps
A brand-new solar system
Appears in her dreams
Creating for her is as easy as it seems.

Here is Mother God who can't help but create even in her dreams. When you think of God the Creator, do you think of God as female or as male.

This image is meant to push us into re-imagining God is a new way. Is her hair tied back by the North Star? Does she paint her toenails? Is she young? Is she old?

Let your imagination soar as you think of God the Mother Creator. Describe her here!

_____

_____

_____

CHAPTER 25

God Created Woman

In the beginning God created Woman. In Her image, God Created Woman.

One of the most famous depictions of God in the Western world is on the ceiling of the Sistine Chapel. It is a representation of God (male) creating Man (not the inclusive word meaning humankind.) It is man as man. It is a glorious image of the masculine God creating the masculine human. God reaches his figure down to the man to pass on the spark of life.

The painting is by a male for a community of religious males.

Where is the other half of humanity represented? She isn't.

This is a masterpiece by Michelangelo in the Sistine Chapel painted between 1508-1512. My image here isn't an amazing illustration like Michelangelo. It's simple to a fault but it's my style. It's cartoon-esque and it gets the point across.

Mother God is soft, curvy and old. She looks like a grandmother. She reaches out her whole hand to Woman, illustrating the old saying:

> Man works from dawn to setting sun
> But woman's work is never done?

Woman needs all the help she can get with all she has to do. Passing on the spark of life like Michelangelo's painting is not enough for the woman. She needs a helping hand from God.

A friend from years ago worked side by side with her husband in the drycleaning business they owned. They worked from 6am to 6pm, side by side. When they got home, he sat down to read the paper while she cooked and cleaned. She explained that he helped her a little; he lifted up his feet so she could vacuum under them.

There was a joke going around about that time that went like this:

> Question: How does a chauvinist clean the toilet?
> Answer: He doesn't. That's women's work.

When I told my husband that joke, he said, "Show me how to clean the toilet!" What a guy! Feminism was raging and men and women's roles started to change in America.

The truth is that all humans need a holy helping hand and a nurturing hand to hold.

How do you feel about this image? Does it ring a bell? Is it shocking? What do you think?

_____

_____

_____

SECTION V

New Images of Jesus and God

After considering these somewhat familiar images of Jesus and God, we are ready to explore some new ideas. Jesus was God, Himself. Others would suggest that he is a human full of God, immersed in God, infused with God. What was Jesus doing that we have not considered before? He was thinking in a new way. He said he came to fulfill the law. What does that mean?

An art teacher explained something about the evolution of art. Before Picasso painted, art was about the expression of things outside of the artist. After Picasso, art became the expression of things inside the artist. So, it is with Jesus and the Law. Before Jesus, the Law was about the outward expression of obeying the rules of God. After Jesus, following the Law was about internal matters, how you thought, how you felt that led to how you acted. Jesus taught a new way to be.

God has been seen interacting with humans in human form. It is difficult to get away from personifying God, seeing God as human form. Now we will explore new images of God as Spirit. How do we see God this way? How would we interact with God this way?

Open your mind and heart to some new ideas, new thoughts, new images of God. See how we can understand God in new ways and, therefore, interact with God differently. Perhaps we can experience God in new ways since God is not limited by body, by time, by space. Consider these different images.

CHAPTER 26

What Would Jesus Do?

This image depicts the story of Jesus and the woman caught in adultery. Jesus is protecting the woman from the stone throwing Jews. No one seems to be asking where the man involved in the adultery is. (That's my bias showing, but not just mine!) ━━━━━━━ ✠ ━━━━━━━

Jesus is wearing the bracelet that was popular among a group of Christians several years ago. It says WWJD, What Would Jesus Do? It was a popular, trendy thing to do. As I look at it now, it strikes me as a vital question for those of us following Jesus today. Asking what Jesus would do is not just about the actions Jesus is taking but is pointing to his inner motivation. In turn, he asks the men who are throwing stones to look at their own motivations that governs their actions. He elevates their awareness by calling out their judgmental personalities. He challenges them to throw the stone if they themselves have never sinned. They are confounded by the confrontation and start leaving, dropping their stones.

Jesus is not giving a new rule but is calling them to a higher awareness, a higher consciousness. Jesus is the melding of physical being and God's Spirit. Jesus calls the people of his day and those who follow him even today into a higher awareness, a higher consciousness, a higher way of being. Jesus calls us to be the New Creation, mentioned by his follower, Paul, in 2 Corinthians 5:17:

> Therefore, if anyone is in Christ, the new creation has come. The old has gone, the new is here.

No one becomes a new creation by following new rules, but by becoming transformed at their core, in their inner being. Connecting with God at our core is what transforms us. I will talk about that transforming practice later and want to elucidate places in scripture where the goal and process of becoming transformed into a new creation are mentioned.

The first place I remember this transformation being mentioned is in the book of Isaiah:

> For my thoughts are not your thoughts, neither are my ways your ways, declares the Lord. As the heavens are higher than the earth, so are my ways higher than your ways and my thoughts than your thoughts. Isaiah 55:9

This is one of the early Scripture that suggest that God is actually a different and higher being than we humans. It isn't until Jesus comes along presenting the New Covenant that God reaches out to humankind to create a new humanity, a new being, a new creation. How does he do it? First, God brings Jesus to us, a proto-type of who we can become. Jesus is a human infused with God and he is different from us. When we are infused with God's Spirit, we can become more like Jesus.

In the Sermon on the Mount, Jesus uses the expression several times:

> You have heard it said…but I say to you…

He refers to murder as a sin, but I tell you, even if you are angry with a person, it is wrong. (paraphrase)

In the whole sermon, he is not talking about sin, per se, he is teaching the people how to become the new creation. He is teaching how to raise the people to a new way of thinking and a new consciousness.

Jesus says he has not come to abolish the law but to fulfill it. He is teaching a new way of being to fulfill the essence of where the law was leading. It's not a new set of rules but is a guideline for a new way of being. The law was an evolution from original lawlessness. Now Jesus describes the next level of evolution. Jesus is saving us from our old way of being.

How do you see your own life changing, perhaps evolving?

_____

_____

_____

Read Matthew 5 and write about your reflections as these teachings relate to you.

_____

_____

_____

CHAPTER 27

Jesus, the Energy Healer

"Who touched me? Who touched me?" Jesus demanded to know!

"But, Teacher, there is a great crowd that surrounds us. They love you; they want your attention. Of, course they all want to touch you!" replied one of the disciples.

"But no, there was someone in particular who touched me. It was intentional for I felt the power go out of me." Luke 8:46

It turns out that a woman had touched him, just the edge of his robe. She wanted to be healed and she thought, "If I just touch the hem of his garment, I will be healed. "She had a bleeding disorder that had gone on for years and she had spent all her money trying to get cured. Jesus was her last hope.

He said, "Power has gone out of me." What did he mean by power?

I believe it was his energy that he felt drained away. Have you ever felt your energy drained?

If you are a parent of little children, you will undoubtedly feel your energy drained out of you. I have two daughters who have little children, 3 years, 5 years, 7 years and 9 years old between them. The most frequent thing I hear them say is, "I'm so tired!" It's true, little children can drain your energy.

Carolyn Myss is a medical intuitive and energy healer and author of the book, *Why People Don't Heal and How They Can. She* explains how energy works in our bodies and the physical and medical dangers of getting our energy constantly drained. When I was sick with Primary Pulmonary Hypertension, I read her book every January for 4 years. Because I was dealing with such a deadly disease, I had to constantly remind myself how to protect myself from energy drain. I recommend this book highly, even for those who are not ill.

The fact that Jesus is aware of his own energy is a very big key to understanding who he was and what he was like.

For instance, when Jesus went walking on the beach and saw the fishermen, he called them to follow him. What was is it that made them respond by throwing down their nets and following him. I believe that they saw, felt, experienced his energy that was different from any other person they met. His energy was powerful, enticing.

When the Roman Centurion came to Jesus and asked him to heal his servant, Jesus offered to come with him. The soldier understood how authority works and that he himself could send a command and knew it would be carried out. He sensed that Jesus's authority could operate at a distance. Jesus's energy was not just present in Jesus's presence, his energy could work at a distance as he wished. The Centurion knew that Jesus's energy was what would heal his servant even from afar. Jesus praised the soldier for his faith, not even being a Jew. Jesus's energy was directed by his will.

The people who heard Jesus speak and saw the mighty acts of healing that he performed declared that he had real authority from God unlike the teachers of the law, the Pharisees. What did they see in Jesus that was different from their own religious teachers? It was his energy!

The book of Luke tells of several times when Jesus healed the people who came to see him and to hear him. Many people came to receive healing. In Luke 5:17 we read "One day He was teaching, and there were some Pharisees and the power of the Lord was present for Him to perform healing."

In Luke 6:19 "And all the people were trying to touch Him, for power was coming from Him and healing them all."

Of course, the gospel writer Luke loved the stories about healing because he was a doctor. And he is very explicit when he writes that God's power was present with Jesus to heal the sick and afflicted people.

What Luke is describing is that the power of God is with Jesus and that power of God heals people. Luke is talking about the energy that lived in Jesus and flowed in Jesus and through Jesus. Jesus got depleted of God's and his own energy when he healed people. His energy, that they describe being from God, is the energy that many people saw in Jesus. That's why they followed him, that's why they wanted to hear him teach as his teaching flowed from the energy of God.

Jesus withdrew from the crowds to pray and be alone. He needed to replenish his energy,

I was a client of an energy healer both when I was sick and after my lung transplant. In total I worked with her, was ministered to by her for 9 years. Energy work will expand and grow in the coming years as a method of healing people both physical and mentally and psychologically. It is a technique beyond therapy. It is a technique that is beyond words. It is a healing technique using energy to heal.

Many people are acquainted with Reiki as a healing practice. It is a method of energy healing. As this model of healing expands and grows, we will come to understand that there is more to healing than medicine, surgery, psycho-therapeutic drugs and talk therapy. None of them can cover the entire spectrum of healing but the different modes can work together to heal a person.

To focus on Jesus as an energy healer is to assert that he is not just using his own energy but is so connected to God, that it is God's energy within him, flowing out of him, that heals people. It is his expanded consciousness, that we refer to as being filled with the Holy Spirit. The term" Spirit-filled" expounds on the experience of a person being connected to and empowered by the energy of God. I have been lucky enough to get to experience the presence of God flowing through followers of Jesus as they pray for my healing.

One of the greatest experiences of the energy of God I ever encountered happened at a John Wimber conference. John was very ordinary. He wore flowered Hawaiian shirts and he confessed to a reporter that, to prepare for a healing service where he would teach and pray, he drank a Diet Coke. When he spoke, it was like ordinary teaching although filled with wonderful stories of people getting healed. Then the "ministry time" came. John announced that the Holy Spirit would come and minister to us. The room, of 5-6,000 attendees, became extremely quiet. It was an exceptional hush. The room got a little cooler. Then, sprinkled through the crowd, individuals began to laugh, or cry, or shake. John said that those individuals were being affected by the Holy Spirit and invited the people close by to just reach out and pray for them. The power of God was present to heal the people.

Through that week I had my own healing experience that was profound. Jesus was with me. It was a most extraordinary experience. But I must tell of my first powerful encounter with God's Presence, God's healing Presence. It was back at home, in Kansas City, at my church, Broadway;

At Broadway Church we offered our own healing conference. Father Francis McNutt, a Catholic priest was a healing minister and author of the book *Healing*. Rev, Tommy Tyson, a Methodist evangelist and Rev. Paul Smith, Southern Baptist pastor, taught about healing. Then, on the last night of the conference, they offered to pray for those who wanted prayer. Most of the attendees came forward for prayer. Francis and Paul prayed in their spirit languages (speaking in tongues) and touching the recipient lightly on the head. 85% of those receiving prayer fell over and "rested in the Spirit." Some people call it "being slain in the Spirit" which is a very brutal and violent way to express this powerful, sweet and tender touch of God.

Of course, I got prayed for, I rested in the Spirit where I was experiencing total blissfulness in God's Presence. It was so lovely and so loving and so powerful in its gentleness. Then an even stranger thing happened. As I was lying there, half-way tucked up under the front pew, I felt this gentle bubbling energy flowing like a gurgling stream flowing over me, from my chin and over my body to my toes. It was such a joyous and delightful feeling, almost like tickling. I began to laugh, laugh out loud, laugh loudly out loud. Then I stopped. Then the people in the pews laughed too. I laughed again, then so did they. I wondered if they were laughing at me. I thought, oh, no. they can't be laughing at me! I felt like I was two blocks away, down the street, relaxing in pure bliss and joy.

Oh, Jesus was an energy healer and still is. We'll look into that further, later.

At the Wimber conference I got in touch with my wound of abandonment from my infancy. On the way to the conference, I had learned that a little boy in my daughter's Kindergarten had died in a horrible accident on the way to school. This brought up my pain of being left when my parents went on vacation. I was nine months old and my babysitter took away my baby bottle. It was devastating for me. This was the pain that was surfacing. The Spirit surfaced the pain and the Presence of God was there to heal.

I was in a class listening to Derek Prince speaking when I felt this powerful emptiness inside and I began to cry. I had to leave the class to go to the bathroom to cry. A deep well of pain opened up and I began to cry harder and louder. One of my friends was passing by and heard me. He recognized me. He couldn't come in to check on me as it was the women's bathroom. How embarrassing to be so public! However, I could not squelch the noisy surfacing of my angst.

I went to my hotel room and screamed into my pillow. How could Jesus be with me when he hadn't been able to prevent this child's death? I screamed until my energy was depleted. As I lay on the bed at last quiet, I heard God speak to me…

"Though you walk through the valley of the shadow of death, I am with you."

It was an amazing, intense experience. I felt the Presence of God fill that emptiness.

Jesus is the human form of God that we can see and feel with our spirits. He contains all the mystical essence of God's energy. He comes to us to heal us. Jesus is an energy healer.

Do you have any experiences of healing whether through counseling, therapy, Reiki, or other?

_____

_____

_____

Are there places in your life that you would like some healing?

_____

_____

_____

Write about these things here.

_____

_____

_____

CHAPTER 28

God as Light

There is a beautiful description of God living in Jesus and in us that is closely connected to the image of God as energy. The image is that God is Light. It is the essence of God living in Jesus and in us that created light for the world. From John 8:12

> When Jesus spoke again to the people he said, "I am the light of the world. Whoever follows me will never walk in darkness, but will have the light of life."

Then, in the book of Mathew, Jesus says to his followers:

> You are the light of the world. A town built on a hill cannot be hidden. Neither do people light a lamp and put it under a bowl. Instead, they put it on its stand, and it gives light to everyone in the house. In the same way, let your light shine before others, that they may see your good deeds and glorify your Father in heaven. Matthew 5:14-16

Many mages of God are poetic and are intended to speak to our hearts more than our minds. In Seminary one of the professors said that to describe a simple concept, it takes very few words. For example, the concept of mud takes one word to describe what it is for us to get the picture. Let's say that the word "mud", in terms of image, covers the ground! Hahahaha, little joke.

The larger and more complex ideas need many descriptors to create the image of the concept. God is probably the most complex idea that we can think of. Therefore, many words, images, metaphors, word pictures are needed to define the concept of God. I don't know if anyone has been totally able to describe everything about God. This book is an effort to describe some of the aspects of God that many hold dear.

I have often observed that, when talking to people about God, their faces seem to "light up". It is also true when people speak of things or people they love, their faces emit a very subtle light. It is the glow of love that expresses itself as light. This is the light of God that lives in our spirits or souls that can become visible on people's faces.

I have wondered what it was that people saw in Jesus that made them follow him. What was it that strong, tough fishermen saw in Jesus that caused them to immediately throw down their nets and follow him? I think that they saw the light of God and felt the energy of God's love that so profoundly affected them that they abandoned their livelihoods to follow Jesus.

I enjoy reading NDEs or Near-Death Experience stories. They are about people who have died briefly, experienced going to the Other Side (Heaven) and returning to talk about it. Many of them experience gentle and powerful love. One person saw a great source of light like a great globe emanating pure love and light. To his understanding, it was the source of all being. What a mystery!

Write some examples of how you have seen the light of God in people.

_____

_____

_____

CHAPTER 29

God as Energy

I went to visit my niece, Meredith, in Lawrence, Kansas, when she was a student at Kansas University. Since we both were following a spiritual path, the topic of conversation quickly dove into the depths of spiritual understanding. Thinking of the subject of what God looks like to different people, I asked her, "What does God look like to you?" Without hesitation she waved her hand in the air in an undulating motion making energy waves.

"You think God is like energy waves?" I asked, just to clarify what she was saying. "Yes!" came the immediate, emphatic reply.

I began contemplating this image of God and found it to be extremely helpful in understanding the essence of God and how God works.

In John 4:24, the gospel writer says,

> God is Spirit and his worshipers must worship him in Spirit and in truth.

What then is Spirit and how do we describe Spirit? I believe Meredith hit on the answer. God is Spirit and Spirit is energy. This description of the essence of God is a new and profound way of seeing God. I love the description of Spirit in the New Testament, comparing it to the wind.

> The wind blows wherever it pleases. You hear its sound, but you cannot tell where it comes from or where it is going. So, it is with everyone born of the Spirit. John 3:8

There was not much science back in Jesus's day so we read the scriptures and find observations about the world and metaphors for God that came from religious contemplation and insight. It is more a modern way to describe the Spirit as energy.

In watching modern day weather reports, weather fronts are often described as energy moving across the land.

Nicola Tesla, electrical engineer, mechanical engineer, inventor and creator of alternating electric current, AC, stated:

If you want to find the secrets of the Universe, think in terms of energy, frequency and vibration.

It is becoming a popular, Avant Garde way of thinking of God as energy. Think of God as the energy of the Universe and as the presence of that energy that lives in us. When we awaken to the Presence of God within us, what Jesus called the "Holy Spirit," we are becoming aware of God's energy within us.

However, there is a difference between energy and God's Energy. This is the great revelation from Jesus and is based on the experience he had of God. And it is the experience his followers have of God as they open to God's presence. God is love. God is energy. God is loving energy. Following is one of my favorite verses from the Bible, from the book 1 John:

> Beloved, let us love one another for love is from God and, whoever loves is born of God and knows God. Anyone who does not love does not know God, because God is love. 1John 4:7-8

The differentiating point is that God is not just energy but is loving energy. Our scientific minds sometimes have a hard time thinking of the physical form that we know as energy combining with the very human notion that is love. Can energy have a personal aspect that we know as love? Yes, this is the great revelation that Jesus had for us. God is energy that is filled with love. To experience God is to experience God as loving energy.

Jesus prayed for all of us when he said:

> My prayer is not for them alone. (Referring to the disciples) I pray for all of those who will believe in me through their message, that all of them may be one, Father, just as you are in me and I am in you. John 17 20=21

When we see God as human form this verse seems to be awkward and not make any sense. How would God become one with a human? If we are imagining God as energy, it makes perfect sense. God's energy can live in us as it did in Jesus. And Jesus's energy lived in God and Win the disciples.

Let's expand this idea to human form and interaction. Can human energy live in someone else? I find that it can. Think about your own relationships. Are there people you know who have happy, fun energy? When they walk in the room does the energy of the room lighten up. Is it more cheerful, more positive? On the other hand, if someone with negative energy connects with you, can you feel your mood change? I had a college friend who talked in a sort of negative whine. I found that, after a few minutes of visiting, I was talking just like her, a soft, low negative whine as if everything was a miserable experience. That is not like me. I am a very positive person. It was her energy that affected me and I started to talk just like her. Her energy became one with me.

If an angry person walks in a room, does the feeling of the room change? My uncle often said that he would hide and watch to see what his dad's mood was when he came home. He was afraid that he would come home angry. People's energy does affect us. We need to be mindful of the affect other people's energy has on us.

I was sick with a formerly fatal disease for five and a half years before my life-saving, death- defying double lung transplant. I had Primary Pulmonary Hypertension. I wore a pump 24/7 that pumped brutal medication directly into my heart every 30 seconds. This medicine kept me alive until transplant and it had painful side effects. Lung transplant is not a cure and not necessarily a fix. I was in a support group of people who were using the pump and the medicine in it, Flolan. I am blessed to live so long. Of all the people I knew in the support group, I am the only one left standing, the only one left alive at this time.

While I was sick, I read a book by Caroline Myss called *Why People Don't Heal and How They Can*. Caroline Myss is a medical intuitive. She reads the energy in people. She can see where stuck energy will create illness in people. It is an amazing gift. I read her book each January while I was sick. I read it four times. There is one take away from the book that served me well.

Myss holds that each day we are given a certain amount of energy. If we are around negative people, they will drain us of the energy that we need to heal our bodies. I took this advice very seriously and worked very hard at protecting my energy. People with negative energy can drain the energy that you need to keep you healthy.

I also got prayed for by people in my church. We prayed in a different way. We prayed by laying hands on people and listening to the Spirit, passing on messages received from Spirit. This kind or prayer sends God's energy into the receiver. This was a tremendous part of healing for me. I appreciate the support I got from all the prayers at Broadway Church. It served as a witness to God's energy at work in and through the people of the church and in me.

I asked for prayer from anyone who would listen. I had to move to St. Louis to wait for my transplant, to be there when my new lungs arrived. I went to get money from my savings account and asked the banker to pray for me. When I picked up my check, she told me that she had immediately called her mother who put me on the church's prayer list. Later I heard from a friend who leads worship internationally. He had been in Brazil and called me to say that he heard that people in Brazil were praying for me. My daughter had been on a trip in Australia and had emailed her contacts there and in the UK to pray for me. I was amazed and humbled by all the prayers on my behalf.

One night a member of Broadway was getting home from work. When she was getting out of the car, she had a strong impression to pray for me and she did. She said she got to church the next Sunday expecting to hear that I had died. But it turned out, she was impressed to pray for me because I was in surgery, the time of transplant was there. She prayed for me during my surgery.

I also saw an energy healer, Dr. Patricia Searing. I saw her for several years before transplant and several years after. She is very gifted in seeing energy, helps move energy and releases places in the body where energy is stuck. I believe that energy healing will become a very important healing mode now and, in the future, as we begin to see everything as energy;

I believe that God's energy was being sent full force to my body for healing and I am eternally grateful for all the love, attention and energy sent my way.

Write your thoughts about seeing God as energy and about the affects of people's energy on you.

_____

_____

_____

SECTION VI

New Images of The Trinity

Most of us who grew up as Christians have been taught about the Trinity. I think most of us didn't get it. God is the One True God and God is Three. What?

In my daughter's wedding ceremony, the officiant was an Episcopalian priest from the groom's home church. Our daughters wanted me, their pastor mother, to be sitting on the front row crying, not performing the ceremony. My daughter is shy and spoke her vows in a very quiet voice until the priest pronounced the end of the vows with "In the name of the Father, Son and Holy Spirit." Lucia blurted out loudly, "Who?" So much for being a minister's daughter. I guess we didn't dwell on teaching the Trinity very much.

The traditional teaching of the Trinity is that the God in three is the Father, Son and Holy Spirit.

Many other phrases seem more evolved like Creator, Redeemer, Sustainer. I like this better.

Paul R Smith presents a new way of viewing the Trinity in his book *Integral Christianity: The Spirit's Call to Evolve (Paragon House 2011)*.

He defines the Trinity in these terms:

> Infinite God in whom we live and move and have our being. Intimate God who is always with us. Inner God: We are the Light of the World.

In his second book about Integral Christianity, *Is Your God Big Enough, Strong Enough, You Enough (Paragon 2017)*, Paul Smith's thinking has evolved further and he defines the Trinity in these terms:

God Beyond us
God Beside us
God Being us

All these new images of the Trinity hold much more meaning about God, the Trinity, and I understand these terms much more. They seem to speak of proximity and function in ways that are clearer and more meaningful.

Let's consider these terms in more depth.

CHAPTER 30

God Beyond Us

It is impossible to think of Creator God in human form since that image could not manage the hugeness of Creation. However, to think of God as energy helps us imagine God as filling the Universe. Facebook postings offer us many ideas about God that stretch our imaginations.

George Steinberg-Caudill shares his understanding God and describes God:

> I do not envision a Creator as a thing or a Being. I envision Creator as Pure Creative Force, an Active Intelligence. Facebook December 30, 2021

Notice that George talks about envisioning God. He is speaking obliquely about an image of God.

My father, his father and two brothers attended college at a small Southern Baptist private school near Kansas City. My grandfather, having been raised on a poor dirt farm by an alcoholic father, put himself through college and medical school and became a general practitioner in my small town. His sons were very bright and attended the same college. The oldest son received a PhD in Chemical Engineering from Massachusetts Institute of Technology. My dad and his other brother became doctors. My dad was a general surgeon and his brother was a urologist, both specialists. They were men of science.

They were all appalled when their favorite science teacher in college got fired for teaching evolution. This created a break between my dad and religion. He didn't speak against the church as we were growing up and my mom held fast and took us to church every Sunday. When I got older, I began to hear about and understand my dad's anger at the church.

In my high school years, I was on my quest to find more of God and asked my dad what he believed about God. I have not forgotten his answer. He said he thought God was "a Higher Intelligence." We would describe my dad as in a Post-Modern stage of development. He believed that science held all the answers to the Universe and that perhaps something else might be out there. That, for him, was Higher Intelligence.

I was touched to learn that, in his last years, the President of the college came to visit him and made a personal plea for reconciliation. It did help heal the wounds of the past.

Anyhow, these descriptors of God seem to help in the understanding of God Beyond Us.

The James Webb telescope, which was launched into space, has just now been sending us pictures of the far reaches of Space, the outer Universe. The images are said to show pictures of early stars that were born shortly after the Big Bang, the beginning of time. The God we know who is Beyond Us is there and here. God, the Great Creating Force, keeps creating.

This image represents the God of the Universe, the God Beyond Us.

Write what this image means to you. How would you describe the God Beyond Us?

_____

_____

_____

CHAPTER 31

God Beside Us

My journey is a Christian journey. I am a follower of Christ. I see that the God Beside Us is Jesus. However, I do not exclude other forms of God Beside Us. There are Angels, Spirit Guides, Ancestors and Loved Ones on the other side. There is the Virgin Mary, Mother of Jesus. There may be other Ascended Masters that walked with people on Earth and still do as Spirit Beings. My writing is, however, about the journey I know as a follower of Jesus. So, I will speak of what I know.

I have several images of the Jesus I know. And I wish to present some different spin on the images we are used to from the stories of the New Testament. Then I have a picture or two from my understanding of Jesus the Mystical Presence. Jesus promised us that he had more to tell us than what the disciples were ready to hear in his days upon the Earth.

I have more to say to you, more than you can now bear. John 16:12

Some of what the Disciples could not hear or understand in that day was how Jesus would be with them after his Crucifixion and Resurrection. Jesus promised that he would be with them (the Disciples) and us through the end of the age. He didn't say how. Now we know and understand that Jesus is with us in his Resurrected body. This is God walking beside us. There are many ways that God walks beside us. May we all learn to open up to the Presence that is always with us.

My friend from elementary school, Monica, told me an amazing story about her dad. He was a scout for the American army during WWII. It was a dangerous job. He had to run across the field between the two opposing forces, between the American army and the German army. It was an area full of artillery fire, bomb holes, barbed wire and danger. He was to find the enemy and report their status and location back to the American commanders. It was an area called "No Man's Land." He was very scared. As he was running across the dangerous field, Monica's dad looked beside him and to his amazement he saw Jesus running beside him. He said to Jesus, "If I come out of this alive and get home safely, I will serve you for the rest of my life." He arrived home safely and served Jesus for the rest of his life.

One of the best kept secrets in Christianity is that Jesus continues to live and be with each of us as a mystical presence. He is with us. We just need to learn how to hear him, see him or experience him being with us. To find Jesus always with us, our loving companion, is life changing!

Have you experienced Jesus being with you, or the presence of another Light Being with you. Write about it here.

If you haven't experienced Jesus's presence with you, and would like to, I invite you to try this simple guided meditation:

Sit quietly in a comfortable place and close your eyes. Imagine that you see Jesus coming toward you and then Jesus sits beside you. If you have a question to ask Him, ask it and then imagine what his response is to your question. Write down the first word, words or phrases that enter your mind. Sit for a minute and let his Presence and his words soak into your heart.

Write about your experience here.

_____

_____

_____

CHAPTER 32

God Being Us

This image of God brings us to ourselves, each of us. If we want to see what God looks like, simply look in the mirror. The Spirit of God lives in each of us. Each of us is made in the image of God and contains a piece of God's creative Spirit within us. Paul Smith's first iteration of the third face of God is "Inner God." In Paul's second iteration the third face of God is "Being Us." Yes, each of us is a piece of God on Earth. We can awaken to this Presence within.

What does that mean?

I saw a cartoon on Facebook that expressed the idea very well. I wish I had copied the cartoon so that I could reprint it here, but I didn't so I will tell you about it. It went something like this:

A young, hip kind of guy was sitting on a park bench with his back pack when Jesus walked up. The guy, with great passion and accusation, asked Jesus a question,

"Why aren't you feeding the hungry children, healing the sick people, stopping the war?"

Jesus responded,

"I was going to ask you the same question!"

God Being Us is the energy of God and the Way of God, the Consciousness of God, that lives in us and empowers us to change the world. We are meant to heal the world. We can believe that each of us is meant to live in the power and presence of God to heal a hurting world.

I, like many others, thrill to the stories shared on the internet, about people who reach out to help others, to help animals, to help the Earth.

There is a story of a young man who decided to clean up a trashed beach in India who found so many people who came to help. What seemed like an impossible task, with many helpers, got done.

There is the group who collects people's used shoes to give to those who don't have shoes. There is the group that shelters and feeds runaway teenagers in big cities.

There is the group that decided to feed the world and is totally funded by donations, not by governments. This group even won the Nobel Peace Prize for their work.

There are those who can't physically participate in these regenerating, renewing activities who can send some money to help the effort.

These are people, whether they realize they are working with God's heart and energy or not, who do good things to help others, to build schools and provide wheelchairs for those who need them.

So, my question to you, gentle reader, can you relate to this image of God? Have you found your purpose since you are made in the image of God?

How do you know what your purpose is? Your purpose and design live in your heart. Are you listening?

As Marie Kondo would say, "What sparks joy in you?" That is the path to follow.

Many people seek to find God's will for their lives as if that will lies outside of themselves. I encourage you to look inside of you. Because the Spirit Energy of God lives within you, God's will is within you. To find it, find out what your passion is, what you love to do. Who and what do you love. Thinking of healing the world, let that love guide you to join in the healing party.

Write about how you see God Being You? What blocks the view?

_____

_____

_____

Write about these things and write about what you could do to help heal the World.

_____

_____

_____

SECTION VII

New Mission

With new images of God and Jesus, perhaps we can consider the mission that Jesus was on. It was conventional wisdom and teaching that Jesus came to seek and save the lost as in the stories of the Lost Coin and the Lost Child. Some teachings say Jesus came to save sinners from Hell. Jesus came to shed his own blood for our sins. This last idea is called the atonement. Jesus came to atone for our sins.

Let's take that last idea, atonement, through its logical process. God sends his beloved son into the world to save those terrible people who are so bad and so sinful they have to have someone save them and pay for their awful sinfulness. They practiced blood sacrifice back in Jesus's time. You bought or brought animals to the temple to pay for your sins. The Priests cut their throats and spilled their blood for the person's sin.

I watched an HBO series years ago called "Rome." The setting was pre-Christian Rome. And, boy, was it pre-Christian. There was no grace, not much love, and massive competition. One woman goes to her temple to pay for a blood sacrifice for her son's success in his career in the Roman Senate. She pays for a bull to be sacrificed. She stands in a space just below the altar. When the bull's throat is cut, the blood gushes out. She is standing underneath and the warm blood pours over her. What an image of being "washed in the blood!"

This is what we are talking about with atonement for sins, being washed in the blood of Jesus. Do we really think this in our day? Does this violent image fit with what we think of God? And who really sacrificed Jesus?

Some say it was Pontius Pilot, some say it was the Jewish leaders who had Jesus killed. Some say it was both. But, going back to what we started with, it was God who killed Jesus. God sent his only son to be the atonement for our sins, the sacrifice for our sins, to be crucified by God like that? That is the logical conclusion of atonement. Is that our image of God? Who wants to be loved by a God like that? How can we be open and vulnerable with an angry, vengeful, killer God? Are we even aware that we are holding that idea of God in our minds and hearts?

Perhaps it is time to consider some other ideas about God and salvation in the 21st century.

If God really is love, how does that change the scenario? How would we see God differently? How do we see Jesus's life differently? How do we see salvation differently?

It's time to consider some new images.

One newer way to think about Jesus is that he is the Christ, the Cosmic Christ. The Christ principle refers to the Divine married with matter the material infused with Spirit. All material things are joined with the Spirit.

Jesus said, "I tell you if they keep quiet (referring to people), the stones will cry out." Mathew 19:40

Matter is infused with God, with the energy of God.

When I returned from St. Louis with my new lungs after transplant, I guess my spirit was vibrating at a high rate. This is what my energy healer observed.

I had a pair of earrings made from rectangles of turquoise. They were lying on the counter in my bathroom. I found myself staring at the turquoise. I could see the energy in them moving, flowing. Even stones are infused with the energy of the Creator.

Jesus is filled with the energy of God. The Resurrected Christ is much more that a man who walked the Earth. Jesus is the personification of Spirit. How would our image of Jesus change, knowing this? Thinking of Jesus this way might change how we understand his mission.

To change our images means to reject what we used to believe. Rejecting our beliefs is a scary thing and it is the way to grow.

I interviewed several people who, I perceived, were actively growing in their faith and their God journey. I found they all had something in common. They were able to reject their former beliefs and sometimes their whole faith system. It is called "Deconstruction."

Actually, Deconstruction is a Spiritual exercise, a way of growing. Doesn't the snake shed his skin because he has gotten bigger? He has outgrown his previous incarnation. Children get new shoes and new clothes because they outgrow their old things. So it is that we can outgrow our belief systems. We cast them off and seek new understandings.

With these new understandings come new images of God and Jesus.

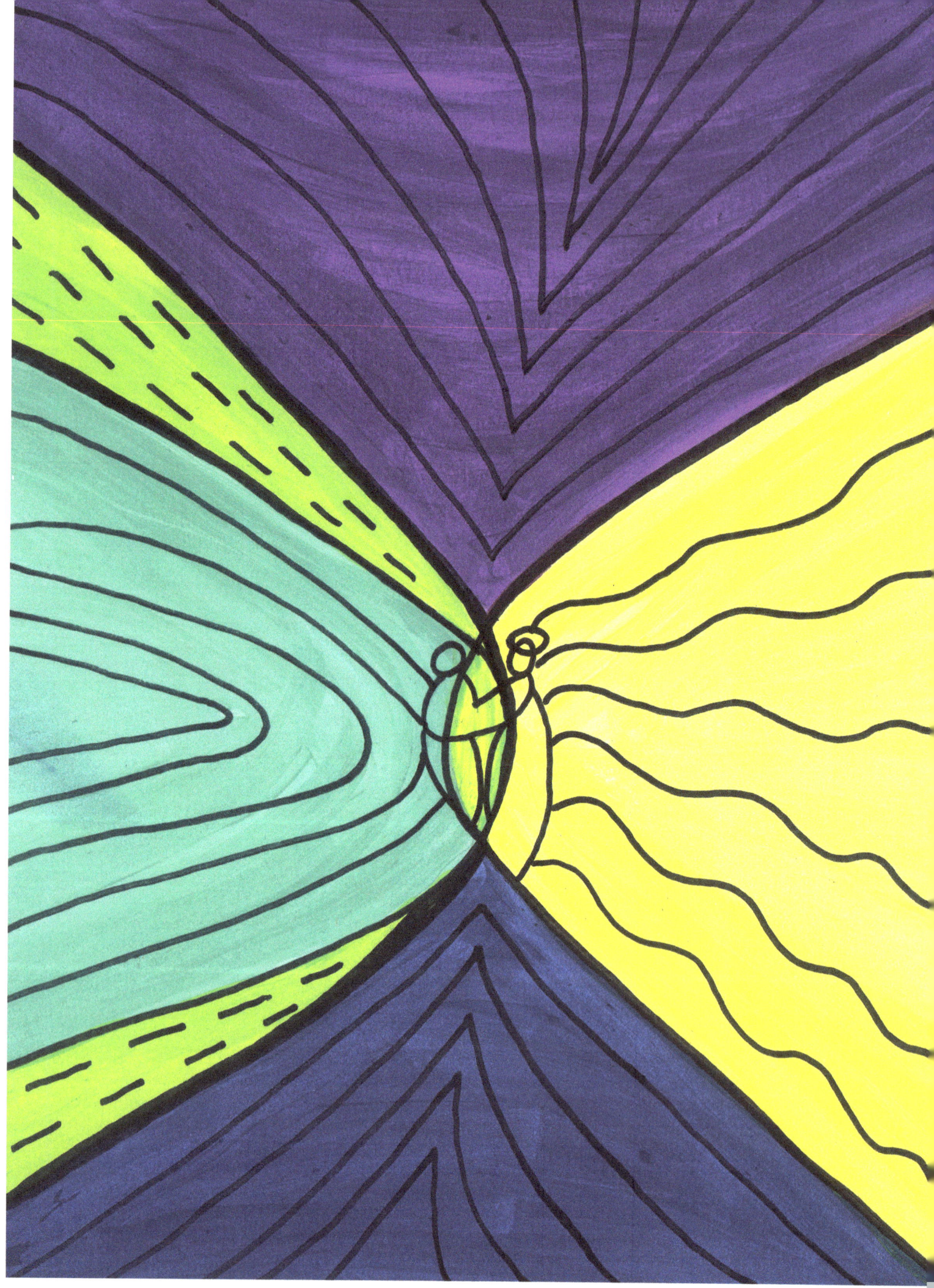

CHAPTER 33

Jesus Raises our Consciousness

This image of Jesus came to me in a vision. It's a picture that popped into my head. I have learned to be able to focus with my spirit for years. I have practiced that "tuning in" for 40 years. I can tell when I am receiving a vision and when I'm just having a thought or memory in visual image form. Most of my paintings come from visions.

When I received this image and painted it, I didn't understand the meaning. At the time I imagined it meant that Jesus was coming from the future (the figure on the right) and humankind (represented in the figure on the left) came from the past. Jesus has come to move us forward to become the evolved form of humans. The ellipticals suggest the movement from the past and toward the future.

In all these years I have been practicing mystical healing prayer and Whole Body Mystical Awakening meditation through Integral Christian Network. I practice the meditation with my small group called a WeSpace group. I continue tuning into mystical messages from Spirit. Now I realize that there is a deeper meaning to the engagement with the mystical journey. To be In Christ means that we are matter connected with the Divine. We are the material being infused with the Divine Spirit. This creates something new, a new kind of human being. We are becoming "the new creation."

If anyone is in Christ, there is a new creation. 2 Corinthians 5:17 New RSV

Mixing matter and Divine energy creates a new creation. We become different. Our consciousness and awareness are changed, are evolved, are more enlightened. I came to realize that this image speaks to us about the New Creation. Jesus comes to save us by redeeming and evolving our consciousness. Living in the energy of God changes us. Since God is Love, God's energy is Love, becoming Love is our goal and our focus. We continue to become Love. Love is the primary focus of an enlightened consciousness.

When Putin invaded Ukraine in the Spring of this year, 2022, the greatest part of the countries of the world objected. No one in the freedom-loving countries wanted that war. I could see such a difference in the reaction of the world than there had been when the United States got involved in the war in Viet Nam. The consciousness of the world is changing and war is more and more heinous to more and more people. As I write, other wars are going on especially on the continent of Africa. Sadly, there is not as much of an outcry to those conflicts. But the world is changing. The consciousness of the people is becoming more advanced.

Here are some interesting scriptures that, as I see them now, are addressing the issue of consciousness.

"For My thoughts are not your thoughts, nor are your ways My ways," declares the Lord. "For as the heavens are higher that the earth, so are My ways higher than your ways and my thoughts than your thoughts." Isaiah 55:8-9

For who has known the mind of the Lord so as to instruct him? But we have the mind of Christ. 1 Corinthians 2:16

To put on the mind of Christ is to think like Jesus did and his mind was infused with the thoughts of God. As Jesus, He was predisposed this way but, being human, he had to act as a human. How did he absorb the mind and consciousness of God? I believe it was by spending time alone with God where he soaked in the energy of God, infused himself with the Presence of God's Spirit. This we can do also.

We must be able to discern the Spirit of God. The way we will always recognize the Spirit of God is that it will feel like love. If you feel a presence that is condemning or negative, if is not God. God always feels loving.

If you learn to listen to Jesus, His words will always feel like love. As we are filled more and more with love, our wounds will be healed and we will begin to think differently. We will think with a foundation of love.

Recently, in meditation I have experienced a new level of God's love. In the Whole Body Mystical Awakening meditation taught in Integral Christian Network, we focus first on our heart center. That is where I feel God's love. Sometimes it becomes very intense, especially when I am expressing my gratitude for all good things I have received. As I have experienced this intense love, I have been able to forgive the people who hurt me in my childhood. I have wanted to do this for a long time. I worked on forgiveness during therapy and in healing prayer. I have set my intention for forgiveness for years. In short, I have done the best that I can.

It wasn't until I felt this intense love that my forgiveness was accomplished. It was like fog being burned off by the sun. It was a negative tension that vanished. When that negativity was released. I noticed that happy memories began to run through my mind. I am so grateful for this healing.

Likewise, when we experience God's intense love for us, we are released into a higher consciousness. We begin to be filled with compassion and our thinking relaxes in the presence of love. In this way we are becoming the new Creation. In this way we are putting on the mind of Christ. Jesus has come to save us from our lack of love.

I don't mean to imply that I have "arrived" at perfection in my spiritual journey. It is a journey and a process. And it is helpful to know when we have made some progress.

I remember when my dear husband, Ken, died. First, I went into shock. I was numb to the reality. It was as if each part of me had to hear the news and hear it at different times. Grief is a process. After two and a half years I started to come out of shock. That's when the crying began in earnest. One night I was sitting in the family room watching TV when I heard the garage door open. My first thought was, "Ken's home." No, it was my daughter arriving and she had her own garage door opener for our house. Bit by bit I was still taking in the news that Ken wasn't coming home.

Growth is like that. Bit by bit our wounds are healed. Bit by bit places in our heart and spirit receive the good news that we are loved unconditionally. Bit by bit the love of God expands in our bodies and in our lives. Bit by bit we become the new creation.

I'll never forget an interview that I saw on TV. My husband loved boxing. George Foreman and Evander Holyfield were heavyweight boxers who were about to engage in a match. I believe it was Foreman who was asked if he hated Holyfield. His amazing response was something like this, "How can I hate him? We are both in Christ. We are brothers." That is an amazing expression of God's love. It comes by being filled with God's love. It is the new Creation, even in men whose job it is to beat the stuffing out of each other.

An important question at this point is, do you have a problem feeling loved? I did. Because of an incident in infancy, I lost my ability to trust. The ensuing depression from that experienced kept me from feeling loved. I had wonderful, fairly normal parents. I knew that they loved me. I knew in my head that they loved me. But in my heart, I could not feel loved.

Reading a book about Ester McCauley by her husband, Bob McCauley, called *A Journey or Trusting,* he tells of Ester's trip to Russian where she finds herself ministering to street children, children on their own, mostly kicked out of their homes by alcoholic, prostitute mothers. They live on the streets, fending for themselves, begging for food and living in the sewer.

One day, after Esther had climbed down into the sewer and saw how the children were living, she climbed back on the street and stood there crying. A child saw her and came over, hit Esther, and demanded to know why she was crying, Esther answered that she was crying because she loved her. The girl hit Esther even harder, claiming, "Nobody ever loved me!" Then the child crawled back into the sewer. She had been rejected all of her life and it was impossible for her to believe that anyone could ever love her.

Even if we have been raised in a loving family, it is difficult to take in God's love. Talking to Jesus and hearing from Jesus helps us begin to take in God's love. I invite you to try it.

Jesus, through His presence with us, changes our awareness and our consciousness so that we know we are loved and can be filled with God's love. This is a powerful experience.

Have you ever felt like Jesus was talking to you? What did it feel like? Write about your experience.

CONCLUSION

We have been taken on a vast journey through many images of God. I hope you have surfaced what has been hurtful in your connection to God and replaced old images of God with new, loving images of God.

Always know that you can discern the Presence of God by how loving it feels. If you "hear" old, hurtful messages of shame, blame, ridicule or criticism, know that that is not God. Perhaps those are old messages we received from childhood. We can carry those old messages for a long time.

We are like the ice cube that, occasionally, jumps out of the freezer onto the floor without notice. It lands on an obscure bit of floor and very slowly, in the presence of warm air, starts to melt. We are like the ice cube, frozen in shame or blame. In the Presence of God's loving warmth, we begin to thaw. It is a process. Sometimes it's a short process and sometimes it's a long process. God's Presence is warm and peaceful, loving and kind, nurturing and healing.

No matter what your image of God is, God always chooses you. Remember, the One you are looking for is looking for you.

ACKNOWLEDGEMENTS

I want to thank all the people who helped me with writing this book:

Those who shared their images of God

Mary Lou Reid, my patient coach with Steve Harrison's "Get Published Now" program

Sarah Kaiser for helping me with all computer problems and solutions

My WeSpace groups for patiently sticking by me while I struggled

For Integral Christian Network for expanding my mystical experiences through this writing

For Dr. Patricia Searing for releasing my energy to be able to write

To Debbie McGuiness, my long-time friend and editor

To Don Milim for his editing advice

For God and Jesus for my breath, my life, and for constant companionship

With Love, Marcia